JEWISH RITUAL

A Brief Introduction for CHRISTIANS

RABBI KERRY M. OLITZKY
AND RABBI DANIEL JUDSON

For People of All Faiths, All Backgrounds

JEWISH LIGHTS Publishing

Woodstock, Vermont

Jewish Ritual:
A Brief Introduction for Christians

2005 First Printing
© 2005 by Kerry M. Olitzky and Daniel Judson

Library of Congress Cataloging-in-Publication Data
Olitzky, Kerry M.
Jewish ritual : a brief introduction for Christians / Kerry M. Olitzky and Daniel Judson.
p. cm.
Includes articles by other authors.
Includes bibliographical references.
ISBN 1-58023-210-8 (quality pbk.)
1. Judaism—Customs and practices. 2. Judaism—Relations—Christianity.
3. Christianity and other religions—Judaism. I. Judson, Daniel. II. Title.
BM700.O433 2005
296.4'5—dc22
2004021971

Grateful acknowledgment is given for permission to print the material contained in this book:
"Keeping Kosher: The Jewish Dietary Laws" © 2005 by Mark Sameth, "Saying Grace and Ninety-Nine Other Blessings throughout the Day" © 2005 by Andrew Vogel, "Going to the Ritual Bath" © 2005 by Debra Nussbaum Cohen. These contributions were based on material previously published in *The Rituals and Practices of a Jewish Life: A Handbook for Personal Spiritual Renewal* © 2002, published by Jewish Lights Publishing.

10   9   8   7   6   5   4   3   2   1

Manufactured in the United States of America
Cover Design: Sara Dismukes

For People of All Faiths, All Backgrounds
Published by Jewish Lights Publishing
A Division of LongHill Partners, Inc.
Sunset Farm Offices, Route 4, P.O. Box 237
Woodstock, VT 05091
Tel: (802) 457-4000   Fax: (802) 457-4004
www.jewishlights.com

For Jerry Levine and Laura Samberg Faino
—KO

And the Reverend Coleman Brown
—DJ

Contents

CONTENTS

PREFACE

JEWISH RITUAL GUIDES the daily life of practicing Jews. It informs the Jewish psyche. It gives concrete expression to Jewish identity, and it reflects deeply held beliefs and value systems. Some Jewish rituals are straightforward. Others are more complicated and require a great deal of explanation and instruction. This book is an introduction to the daily or weekly Jewish rituals that are best known and most practiced. Each chapter introduces you to a specific ritual. For those interested in exploring these rituals in greater depth, we have included a list of suggestions for further reading at the end of the book. Although we have limited the number of Hebrew words in each chapter, and have defined them as we have used them, we have also included a glossary at the back of this volume.

Judaism can be confusing because of the differing movements within Judaism and their divergent approaches to Jewish practice. Further, in the past few years, Judaism has been undergoing a small transformation as its liberal wing moves toward a more traditional approach to Jewish ritual practice. Previously, the more liberal movements often modified or abandoned certain rituals to reflect their particular theology.

The idea that ritual can be changed and adapted may also be confusing to some Christians (and some Jews as well). While there are established rules for ritual practice (emanating from the body of Jewish law called *halakhah*), there is also a great deal of flexibility in the implementation of Jewish ritual, as well as opportunities for personal and creative expression.

We have written all the chapters except where a different author is noted, and each chapter, no matter the author, includes a variety of approaches to many of the rituals covered in this book. We have also tried to compare and contrast each ritual with relevant Christian religious practices to deepen their meaning for Christian readers.

ACKNOWLEDGMENTS

WE ARE GRATEFUL to Jon Sweeney of Jewish Lights Publishing for inviting us to prepare this volume, motivated by the successful publication of our first collaborative effort, *The Rituals and Practices of a Jewish Life: A Handbook for Personal Spiritual Renewal* (Jewish Lights). No book would be complete without the thoughtful guidance and support of the publishers, Stuart and Antoinette Matlins, whose optimistic and inclusive Jewish communal vision continues to inspire us. Grateful to them both, we are humbled by the opportunity to share their passion for Judaism and Jewish ritual with others and be elevated heavenward as a result. We also thank the many staff members of Jewish Lights Publishing who, with great care and compassion, gently moved this project along from concept through production and distribution. In particular, we thank our editor, Emily Wichland, who takes loving care with each word on the printed page.

We also thank the many people who read sections of this book, particularly those in the Christian community. In particular, we express our appreciation to Rich Basile, Kelley Connolly, the Reverend Michael Doyle, and the Reverend Dr. Kirk Smith.

We thank our families and children—Sandy Falk, Naftali and Maayan Falk-Judson and Sheryl, Avi, and Jesse Olitzky—

who share with us a vision for a better world as shaped by the words of the Divine.

We must thank the Holy One of Blessing who has brought us to this day and constantly inspires us to do this sacred work together.

Rabbi Daniel Judson
Rabbi Kerry ("Shia") Olitzky

INTRODUCTION:
WHY WOULD CHRISTIANS BE
INTERESTED IN THE RITUALS
OF JUDAISM?

IN SOME WAYS, this book marks a watershed moment. Because there are enough Christians today interested in Jewish rituals to warrant the publication of this book, we have reached a dramatic turning point in the way Jews and Christians see each other. It was precisely Jewish rituals from which the early church broke away. The apostle Paul vehemently rejected the detailed laws of Jewish observance, such as the many rules surrounding keeping kosher, and for almost two millennia this basic disapproval of Jewish ritual has been a part of the church.

But today we live in a far different world than the generations before us. The extent to which religions come into contact with each other is historically unprecedented. Jews and Christians not only live next door to each other, they often live with each other. You may be reading this book because you yourself or someone in your family is engaged in a relationship with someone who is Jewish. You may be seeking to better understand new Jewish parents-in-law, a new Jewish brother-in-law or daughter-in-law, or maybe a new Jewish wife or husband.

Some Christians may delve into this book out of an interest in Christian history. You may want to learn more about the tradition out of which Christianity sprang. In exploring Jewish rituals, you will find that some are profoundly similar to Christian rituals, such as the *mikvah* and baptism (see chapter 9). Not only may this knowledge provide you with an understanding of Jewish ritual, but it may also give you a deeper understanding of your own Christian faith as well. We should note that there is a lot of precedent in Christian history for just this type of religious inquiry. We know, for example, that the Pilgrims were fascinated with Hebrew and studied with the rabbis of Holland to learn the language so that they could read and translate the Hebrew Scriptures for themselves.

Some Christians may be coming to this book for yet a third reason. We live in a syncretistic age; that is, an age in which there is a great deal of borrowing and swapping between cultures and religions. Judaism and Christianity have always borrowed ideas from each other and have even adapted rituals from each other, but today, with the advent of the Internet, this trend has increased exponentially. You may be turning to this book with the intention of finding a practice that speaks to you, a practice you could adopt as your own.

Jewish mysticism contends that there are basic fissures in the fabric of the world—broken places where God's presence cannot be felt. It is the obligation of each individual to perform *tikkun* (repair), healing acts to mend these broken places of the world. The history of Jewish-Christian relations is such a place of brokenness. It is in need of millions of acts of mending. We fervently hope that the writing and reading of this book will be one such act, one small *tikkun* in this process, allowing Jews and Christians to see each other's religion with greater clarity and greater respect.

A Note on the Text

ACCORDING TO JEWISH TRADITION, the first five books of the Bible were given as the Torah (or written law) to the Jewish people on Mount Sinai. An oral law was given at the same time, alongside the written law. While passed down orally from one generation to the next, this oral law was originally written down in two sections. The first section is called the Mishnah. The second section (which serves as an overlay to the first section) is called the Gemara. Together, both sections form the Talmud. Except where noted otherwise, all of our quotations from the Talmud are taken from the Babylonian version.

Throughout this book we have quoted from and translated the Hebrew Bible, which sometimes orders its books differently than does the canonized Christian version of Hebrew Scriptures (the so-called Old Testament). At times, it also numbers its chapters and verses slightly differently. All quotations from the Bible are our own translations, sometimes adapted from the Jewish Publication Society translation.

1

OBSERVING THE SABBATH

Remember the Sabbath to sanctify it.

—EXODUS 20:8

Keep the Sabbath day to guard it.

—DEUTERONOMY 5:12

THE BASICS

MAYBE IT IS MIDDLE AGE, but I can actually feel my body beginning to shut down as I make my way home each Friday afternoon in anticipation of Shabbat (the Sabbath). I can push all week long—early mornings and late nights—but, come Friday, I am ready to completely unwind. It isn't just the bodily rest that I crave; it is the deep spiritual nourishment that the Sabbath provides. By separating myself from the frenzy of the world that surrounds me all week long, I can focus on the needs of my soul throughout Shabbat. It is an island away from secular intrusions on my spiritual world.

Shabbat is unlike any other day. For starters, it is twenty-five hours long. It begins on Friday afternoon eighteen minutes before sunset and goes through Saturday night after the stars have come out. Because the start of Shabbat changes each week with the changing time of sunset, I am forced to admit that I am not in control of the world around me. So I consciously let go and let God lead the way to holiness for me.

The Sabbath begins with the lighting of candles and the short blessing marking the time as sacred and special. This is followed by a kiddush prayer (over wine or grape juice) to sanctify the day, the blessing of children and spouse, a festive meal with singing, and *Birkat Hamazon,* a prayer of thanksgiving or Grace after Meals, as it is sometimes called. The basic elements are repeated, in a modified form, at Shabbat lunch on Saturday and at a third meal (known by its Hebrew translation, *seudah shelishit*) that takes place in the late afternoon or early evening depending on the time of year, as well as with worship and study along the way. The Sabbath concludes with a ritual called *Havdalah,* as explained on pages 11–12 later in this chapter.

The primary goal in observing the Sabbath is to limit the intrusion of the workaday world so that we can focus on the more important issue of spiritual renewal. The Rabbis (that is, the Rabbis of ancient times—with a capital *R*) established prohibited labors on the Sabbath as a guide. They deduced these prohibited activities from the various tasks that were required to build the ancient Tabernacle. In this way, they transformed the idea of building sacred space into building sacred time.

—KO

BROAD STROKES OF SABBATH OBSERVANCE

My friend Rachel and my ultra-Orthodox cousins both observe the Sabbath, but they do so in different ways. My cousins in Williamsburg, Brooklyn, observe the Sabbath by following a vast array of rules as to what they can and cannot do. They spend all Friday cooking and cleaning, readying themselves for the Sabbath when they will not use electricity, the television, or the computer, and they will not spend any money. Rachel observes the Sabbath as well. She wakes up on Saturday morning and goes to the gym to work out. When she gets home, she spends time with her husband and then heads for her favorite bookstore, where they have wide comfortable chairs, good coffee, and don't mind people spending a few hours reading. She believes that the Sabbath is about giving oneself joy in life, and few things bring her as much pleasure as an afternoon browsing through books.

My cousins in Williamsburg would never acknowledge that Rachel was observing the Sabbath by working out and going shopping at the bookstore. On the other hand, Rachel would hardly equate her Sabbath ritual with my cousins' extensive Sabbath preparations. But the Jewish observance of the Sabbath runs the gamut from my cousins' all-encompassing Shabbat to Rachel's jogging and caffe latte.

For my cousins, the observance of the Sabbath is anchored in traditional Jewish law. The laws concerning Shabbat were laid out in the Mishnah (part of what is called the oral law). The Rabbis of the Mishnah tried to define what constitutes "work." In various places in the Bible, we are told that we should observe the Sabbath as rest because God rested on the seventh day after creating the world. But the Bible does not detail precisely what "rest" or "work" encompasses. The Bible does tell us about the poor laborer who was caught gathering wood on the Sabbath and summarily stoned for working on the holy day. But besides gathering wood and lighting a fire, we are given no further information about what constitutes work. The Rabbis of the Mishnah thus attempt to spell out "work." They take their lead from the work that was required to build the Tabernacle that the Israelites brought with them during their desert journey from Egypt to Canaan, and deduce thirty-nine categories of work, what they call *melakha*. While we might not consider them part of our daily work, these categories include planting, tearing, putting two letters together, building, and mixing. Most of the activities on the list are agricultural tasks that reflect the farming society in which the Rabbis lived.

The traditional Sabbath my cousins observe is rather stringent. Following the categories of prohibited work (and later work-related activities that were added to the list), you are not permitted to drive or carry anything outside of your own private space—that means the home (although the Rabbis allowed for private space to be expanded artificially by stringing a wire called an *eruv* around the area—similar to the way power lines are strung—to expand the area in which an individual could carry objects outside the home). You are not permitted to use the phone, to go online, to watch movies, or to shop. You cannot cook, write a letter, or garden. While the list seems overwhelming, the goal is simply to ensure that you separate yourself from any activity that could potentially be work or lead you to work. Thus, you can't even touch certain items, even if you have no intention of using them.

They may appear burdensome, but these restrictions are merely an attempt to help create holy space, by keeping you from the ordinary, the everyday, and elevating you to a more sacred and spiritual plane. By limiting what you are permitted to do, traditional Shabbat restrictions force you to give up the illusion of "control" over your life. Instead, you strip down to life's essentials by getting together with others to eat and talk and celebrate just being alive. If you can't rush off to the shopping mall or work just a little bit more, you can create sacred space in your life to linger over conversation, or to be intimate—physically and spiritually—with your partner. You are able to enter into what Rabbi Abraham Joshua Heschel, considered one of the great rabbis of the twentieth century, calls a "sanctuary of time." This is a period in which you stop trying to change the world (an important part of Jewish ethical life) and simply strive to be in harmony with it.

Unlike my cousins, Rachel does not believe that such strict rules are necessary to experience the Sabbath. For her, observing the Sabbath is much simpler. The Rabbis must have anticipated her attitude when they wrote, in a well-known midrash (a rabbinic legend that explains passages in the Bible), "Shabbat was given only for pleasure." For Rachel, the Sabbath is about doing things that bring her pleasure: working out, reading, drinking coffee. She believes that as long as she is mindful that the activities she is doing are connected to Shabbat, then she is indeed observing the Sabbath.

My cousins and my friend represent two opposing ends of the Shabbat observance spectrum. Rachel sees the Sabbath as being primarily about bringing joy to your life without any specific rules or regulations; my cousins, by contrast, see the Sabbath as a way to set apart one day of the week for complete rest from the world, which, to them, can be accomplished only by following a specific set of guidelines.

Since most of us live somewhere in between, both seem right to me. I try to keep both of these Sabbaths at once. I try to do things that bring me joy while simultaneously recognizing that withdrawing myself from daily activities frees me to experience inner peace in a profound way. Practically, I observe two primary rules to separate myself during Shabbat from my regular days. First, I do not spend any money. This keeps me away from movies, shopping malls, and restaurants. Second, I do not turn on my computer, which keeps me from the temptation to check e-mail, pay a bill online, or finish up that essay or lesson I am preparing.

Franz Rosenzweig, the great Jewish philosopher, said, "The Sabbath is a world revolution." It may seem odd to call the Sabbath revolutionary, since nothing seems less "revolutionary" than a three-thousand-year-old idea. But even if the observance of the Sabbath in our time is not revolutionary, it is, indeed, subversive. There is something subversive about consciously withdrawing from worldly preoccupations. While much of our culture is engaged with commerce, Shabbat is an opportunity to choose not to take part in that world—even if that means just spending Shabbat evening drinking wine with the one you love, reading Harry Potter with your child, or being still by yourself and enjoying the solitude.

For some people, it is almost incomprehensible to spend Friday night or Saturday not going out or working. Occasionally, when I see a listing for a concert or a show, or I am invited to a friend's party on a Friday night, I momentarily regret my decision not to participate in these activities on the Sabbath. But, for me, the spiritual discipline of not spending money and not socializing in ways not related to the Sabbath provides me with benefits that transcend the transient joy of a party or a movie. In consistently observing the Sabbath, you can feel an "intuition of eternity," as Heschel calls it. For me, this is not about a magical or mystical experience. Rather, this feeling of Shabbat—set apart from the other days—suffuses me with a profound appreciation for slowing down, for resting, and for appreciating the blessing of time itself.

—DJ

CREATING THE ISLAND OF SHABBAT

To create space in your life to observe the Sabbath—that island of peace—you have to have some sense of boundaries. It can be hard to create that island, especially if you are very busy all week long. A friend told me that the sole rule of Shabbat that she and her family observe is to have Friday night dinner together, the only meal of the week when they are together. At dinner, they go around the table and describe their week—the difficulties they had, and the blessings they felt. Sometimes it is a wonderful experience from the moment they all sit down together; sometimes her teenage daughter opens up in a way she never does during the rest of the week.

But on other occasions her husband will call and say he is going to be late, and her daughter will grumble as she sits down, in that pouty-teenager sort of way, about having to make blessings and share time with her parents. Sometimes the strain of getting together makes everyone mad at each other right through the blessings and into the salad. And if the point of the Sabbath is relaxation, Shabbat appears to be "backfiring." But, she says, eventually, sometime between the main course and dessert, when everyone has decompressed long enough to realize that the goal is to be together just this one time a week, they relax, and the transcendent experience of Shabbat sets in.

THE SABBATH AS A SYMBOL OF ONENESS

The Ten Commandments appear twice in the Hebrew Scriptures. Their revelation at Mount Sinai is first recorded in Exodus and then retold in Deuteronomy. The Book of Exodus says that you should "remember" the Sabbath and keep it holy. Deuteronomy tells us to "guard" the Sabbath. To Jewish readers of the Bible, this slight semantic difference looms large. Commentators see in this shift of wording two ways of observing the Sabbath. "Guarding" Shabbat means adhering to the myriad restrictions imposed by Jewish law that ensure that you will not work. This represents the passive aspect of Shabbat—refraining from work. "Remembering" Shabbat, by contrast, means taking positive actions to increase the joy and peacefulness in your life.

Jewish tradition commemorates the two times the Ten Commandments appear in the Bible by lighting two candles on the Sabbath. This is just one of a number of rituals on Shabbat, which, like the animals on Noah's ark, come in pairs. "Everything pertaining to Shabbat is double...." (*Midrash Tehillim* on 92:1). Customarily, two loaves of challah (braided egg bread) are used to represent the double portion of manna that fell on Friday for the Israelites to gather when they were wandering in the wilderness for forty years. We even have two souls on the Sabbath: The Talmud says that on Shabbat we receive a second soul, which goes away at the conclusion of Shabbat (*Betzah* 16a). The Talmud also says that a pair of angels escort a person home from the synagogue on the eve of the Sabbath (*Shabbat* 119b).

Yet for all the doubling, Shabbat is ultimately about two becoming one. For the mystics it was the male and female aspects of the Divine uniting. The Zohar, the primary text of Kabbalah (the practice of Jewish mysticism), says that just as the male and female aspects of the Divine unite above, so they also unite below in the mystery of the Oneness. Some take this to mean that we should engage in the "double mitzvah" of Shabbat—that is, to make love with our partner, the ultimate expression of two becoming one. The Rabbis even say that the two times where the Ten Commandments appear in the Bible, God actually spoke them at the exact same time, some-how, in the mystery that is the Oneness of God. The Sabbath prayer song *Lekhah Dodi* (Come, My Beloved) says this quite simply: *Shamor vezakhor bediboor echad,* God uttered the words *guard* and *remember* as one word.

SABBATH CANDLELIGHTING CUSTOMS

Two candles are usually lit for the Sabbath. They represent the two times the commandment to observe the Sabbath is given in the Bible, and, specifically, the two different words, *shamor* (guard) and *zakhor* (remember) that begin the commandment. But explanations for this custom abound, and some families go beyond this two-candle minimum. Some add a candle for each child. Others use a third candle to represent all their children. Because of the significance of the number seven in Judaism (for example, the seven days of creation), other customs include the lighting of seven Sabbath candles.

One classic Jewish image is a woman lighting two Sabbath candles before the sun sets. She closes her eyes intently and circles her hands in the air, as if to draw the energy of the candles into her, and she recites the traditional blessing.

The commandment to light candles is meant for men as well as women, but the custom evolved for women to light the candles because they are more closely associated with the home. In liberal Jewish circles, men sometimes light Sabbath candles, yet the custom of women lighting candles still holds sway, even in Jewish communities where women are rabbis and lay Jewish leaders.

After the candles are lit, the blessing is said over the Sabbath candles with eyes closed. Customarily, the person lighting candles adds a silent blessing for the family. Why are the eyes closed? The answer is not so simple. My mother used to say that no custom in Judaism is ever "so simple." Jews usually say a blessing before performing an act; for example, you say the blessing over bread *before* eating bread. But the blessing over the candles marks the beginning of the Sabbath, and on the Sabbath it is forbidden to create light. So you would be violating the rules of Shabbat by saying the blessing and then lighting the candles. Yet, in this case, you need to say the blessing before the act is done. So it became the custom to light the candles with the eyes closed so you wouldn't see the light while reciting the blessing. When you lower your hands from your eyes, it is as if you had said the blessing before the candles were lit.

Tradition prescribes that you light candles eighteen minutes before sunset. The Sabbath commences officially at sunset, but the lighting of candles marks the beginning of the Sabbath for those who lit the candles. The candlelighting is done early, both to provide a cushion of time so you won't accidentally light candles after sunset, and because it is difficult to determine exactly when sunset occurs.

Sabbath light is the symbol of joy and harmony. We are drawing this joy and harmony into ourselves and our home. The Sabbath is also imagined as a bride and the waving of the hands ushers the bride into the house.

The Book of Proverbs says, "The soul of a person is the light of God." After the candles are lit, many people take a moment to reflect on the soul, our inner being, who we are in the world, and how our inner light is connected to God's divine light.

OTHER SHABBAT RITUALS

Here is a very brief sketch of the rituals associated with each time period of Shabbat.

Friday Night Dinner/Friday Night

The Talmud says that a person is accompanied home on Friday night by two angels who guard the way (*Shabbat* 119b). Traditionally, families light Shabbat candles, and then the men go to synagogue for a brief prayer service called *kabbalat Shabbat* (welcoming the Sabbath). They come home and the Shabbat evening ritual begins with the kiddush (a blessing, said over wine, that sanctifies the day) and the *motzi* blessing over challah bread. This is followed by a Sabbath meal.

Sabbath Day

Shabbat morning is traditionally a time when people go to the synagogue. The highlight of the service is the reading of the Torah (the first five books of the Bible) portion of the week, which is designed to help us reexperience the revelation at Sinai. It was at Sinai that the ancient Israelites entered into a covenantal relationship with God on their way through the desert. Sinai became the turning point for the Israelites and marked their move from a slave people to a free nation. We go to the synagogue to pray, to be with friends, and to celebrate the joys of Jewish community.

Saturday Sunset: Havdalah

Just as the Sabbath is ushered in with a ritual act of candle-lighting, so we leave the Sabbath with a similar ritual act that involves light. It is a bittersweet time. It is also a time steeped in mystery as the daylight slips into darkness. We hate to let go of the Sabbath. This brief ritual marks the end of the Sabbath and helps us to make the transition back into the workaday world—even though most of us don't work on Saturday night or Sunday. The *Havdalah* ritual takes place at sundown, some twenty-five hours after lighting Sabbath candles. This lovely, simple ceremony includes wine, a special braided candle, and fragrant spices. The ceremony is a sensuous experience of enchanting lights and sweet-smelling aromas.

The *Havdalah* ceremony begins with a song that invites the prophet Elijah—who will herald the coming of the Messiah, according to Jewish tradition—into our midst. It continues with a paragraph taken from the Psalms that speaks of God as the source of redemption, followed by four brief blessings. The first blessing is said over wine. The second one is recited over spices—a reminder of the sweet fragrance of the Sabbath and a way to revive the soul, which has been diminished as a result of the Sabbath's departure. Then comes a blessing said over the multiwicked *Havdalah* candle that acknowledges the creator of the flame. The candle mirrors the intertwining of the Sabbath day with the rest of the days of the week. Finally, a blessing is said praising God for helping us to distinguish between various things in our lives, particularly the holy and the secular. The wine is sipped and then the candle is extinguished in the wine. People wish each other a "good week" and then return to their daily activities, which have been postponed for the Sabbath.

CHRISTIAN PARALLELS TO JEWISH SHABBAT OBSERVANCES

The Sabbath in Christian tradition has much in common with Jewish observance. While the modern Christian church does not typically follow the minutely detailed set of Shabbat prohibitions, traditionally Christians also did not work or do anything frivolous, such as going to the movies, on Sunday (the day that most Christians associate with the Sabbath). This tradition was reflected in the local "blue laws" in the United States, designed to keep most stores closed on Sunday. Mark Twain once joked, "The day was as long as a Protestant Sunday." During the Sabbath day, a Christian's goal was similar to a Jew's: to set aside time for meditation, to enjoy refreshment, and to spend time with family. Pressure from popular culture has placed many church services in conflict with civic groups, sports practices, and other diversions on Sunday morning. Recently, though, Christians have been rediscovering the importance of keeping the Sabbath for their spiritual health.

One aspect of the Sabbath where Judaism and much of Christianity have parted ways is on what day Shabbat should be observed. The Catholic Church and most Protestant churches observe the Sabbath on Sunday in commemoration of the resurrection of Jesus, which, according to the Gospels, happened on the first day of the week; that is, on Sunday. Some Christians, however, such as Seventh-Day Adventists, cite passages such as Acts 18:4, which says that Paul went to synagogue every Sabbath, to claim that the Saturday Sabbath was observed by Paul and should therefore still be observed on that day.

The difference between the observance of Sabbath days has historically caused difficulties for Jews economically. If Jews observed the Sabbath on Saturday and worked for a non-Jewish employer, there was tremendous pressure to work on Shabbat. This led to the radical suggestion by some nineteenth-century Reform rabbis in Germany to move the Jewish Sabbath to Sunday, to allow Jews to observe Shabbat without being pressured economically. In America, some rabbis in the late nineteenth century called for a five-day workweek, precisely so both Jews and Christians could observe their respective Sabbath days. As America moves to a seven-day week of commerce, with stores open every day, both faiths now suffer from the incessant call of commercialism.

2

KEEPING KOSHER: THE JEWISH DIETARY LAWS

Rabbi Mark Sameth

Do not boil a kid in its mother's milk.
—EXODUS 23:19, EXODUS 34:26,
AND DEUTERONOMY 14:21

THE BASICS: IS IT KOSHER?

THE SPIRITUAL DIETARY DISCIPLINE that guides what Jews eat is known by the general term *kosher*. The word *kashrut* (Hebrew for "kosher") means "appropriate" or "fit." Kosher food, therefore, means food that is proper or fit for consumption. The dietary laws are spread throughout the first five books of the Bible; readers are unable to find them in one place or even one section. They include the prohibition against the eating of *trefah* (in Yiddish, *treyf*—a term used to refer to all food that is not kosher), flesh torn by beasts in the field (Exodus 22:30), and the prohibition against slaughtering an animal and its young on the same day (Leviticus 22:28). Moses Maimonides, a twelfth-century rabbi who fled Spain for Egypt and is considered the most important Jewish philosopher of all time, saw this prohibition as a precautionary measure in order to avoid slaughtering the young animal in front of its mother. He thought that animals felt grave pain and argued that there is no difference between the pain experienced by people and that of animals.[1]

As part of the dietary laws, there is also an injunction to chase a mother bird away before taking her eggs (Deuteronomy 22:6). Regarding this requirement, Maimonides wrote, "If the Law takes into consideration these pains of the soul in the case of beast and birds, what will be the case with regard to the individuals of the human species as a whole?"[2] By maintaining our sensitivity to the feelings of other creatures, these laws, in the words of Rabbi Samuel Dresner, have as their purpose "the teaching of reverence for life."[3]

But there is more: a prohibition against eating anything that has died a natural death (Deuteronomy 14:21), a prohibition against boiling a kid in its mother's milk (which appears three times in the first five books of the Bible—Exodus 23:19, Exodus 34:26, and Deuteronomy 14:21), a prohibition against eating blood, and a direction to eat only animals that both chew their cud and have cloven hoofs (hence, the well-known prohibition against eating pigs and pork). Certain animal fats must be removed, as must the sciatic nerve. Only fish that have both fins and scales are permitted; shellfish are not considered kosher, nor are some birds. With the exception of four locusts, insects and swarming things are also forbidden.

Over time, the Rabbis extended the terse dietary laws to further ensure humane slaughter (which is called *shechitah*), to prohibit the consumption of milk and meat at the same meal, to prohibit the eating of fowl and milk at the same meal, and to make practical the requirement to keep separate dishes and utensils for dairy meals and for meat meals. They also determined that foods such as fruits, vegetables, grains, nonprohibited fish, and eggs, which are neither dairy nor meat, are neutral (called *pareve*) and may be eaten with either meat or dairy products.

Today, individual rabbis (and groups of rabbis) certify kosher meat and fowl. Processed foods, too, are often certified as kosher, meaning all the ingredients used in their production are also kosher. Foods that carry a stamp of approval, or *hekhsher,* on the package—a symbol such as a *K,* a *K* or a *U* inside a circle, or a *K* inside the Hebrew letter *kaf*—are all certified kosher by individual rabbis or local community boards of rabbis who supervise the observance of proper dietary practices for the community.

THE BIBLICAL IDEAL

While the Bible does not require people to maintain a vegetarian diet, it does consider vegetarianism ideal. In the Garden of Eden, God tells the first humans, "Here, I give you all plants that bear seeds that are upon the face of the earth, and all trees in which there is tree fruit that bears seeds, for they shall be for eating for you" (Genesis 1:29). According to the Bible, not only were humans intended to be herbivores, but so were animals. "And also for all the living things of the earth, for all the fowl of the heavens, for all that crawls upon the earth in which there is living being—all green plants for eating; it was so" (Genesis 1:30). Permission to eat meat would not come until ten generations later. After the Flood, when only Noah and his family are left of the generation that had "gone to ruin" (Genesis 6:12), a concession is made. "All things crawling about that live, they be to you for eating, as with the green plants, I now give you all" (Genesis 9:3). But the concession is not unconditional permission. There is one important proviso: "However, you are not to eat flesh with its life, its blood!" (Genesis 9:4).

From the biblical laws of kashrut, Judaism derives two important ethical principles: the prohibition against causing needless suffering (in Hebrew, *tzaar ba'alei chaim*) and the prohibition against wanton destruction (in Hebrew, *bal tashchit*). The prohibition against causing needless suffering to any living creature derives from teachings in Hebrew scriptures, including the following: the injunction not to plow with a weak animal yoked to a strong one, as the weaker one will wear itself out trying to keep up (Deuteronomy 22:10); the prohibition against muzzling an ox while it is threshing grain, but rather allowing it to eat at will (Deuteronomy 25:4); the requirement to rest your animals on the Sabbath (Exodus 23:10); the requirement to chase a mother bird from the nest before gathering her eggs or her chicks (Deuteronomy 22:6–7); and the prohibition against slaughtering an animal and its young on the same day (Leviticus 22:28).

The prohibition against wanton destruction or wastefulness derives from Deuteronomy 20:19, which reads:

> When you besiege a town for many days, waging war against it, to seize it, you are not to bring ruin on its trees, by swinging an ax against them, for from them you eat. You are not to cut them down—for are the trees of the field human beings, [able] to come against you in a siege?

From this, the Rabbis deduced many teachings against wanton destruction and in favor of conservation. "A palm tree," they wrote, "producing even one piece of fruit may not be cut down" (*Bava Kamma* 91b). Regarding the consumption of meat, we are cautioned in the Talmud, "You should not eat meat unless you have a special craving for it." It is stated on the same page that a parent should not "accustom a child to flesh" (*Chullin* 84a).

RABBINIC KASHRUT

When people use the term *kosher,* they usually mean the dietary laws as shaped by the Rabbis—a system that begins with the Bible, but then is amplified and/or expanded upon by later commentators. For example, the Bible says that in slaughtering an animal one must "pour out its blood, and cover it with the dust" (Leviticus 17:13), but is not explicit about how that should be done. So the Rabbis who wrote the Talmud specify how to slaughter humanely, laying out precise rules on the topic.

Another example of the difference between the Bible's dietary laws and how they have been amplified by the Rabbis is the separation of milk and meat. The Bible says simply that you should not boil a kid in its mother's milk. But the Rabbis expanded this verse in the Bible to mean that you should not mix any milk products with any meat products. This is why people who keep kosher (not all Jews keep kosher) have two sets of dishes, so that plates on which meat has been served are not used for serving dairy foods. These plates are even stored separately so that they do not touch each other. It is quite a leap to go from not boiling a kid in its mother's milk to not eating cheeseburgers and having two different sets of dishes, but the Rabbis of the Talmud were concerned about individuals accidentally trespassing on biblical laws. Their response to this fear was to expand the laws (in the language of the Talmud, "to make a fence around the law") to avoid the possibility that someone might accidentally break a biblical commandment.

An entire tractate of Talmud (approximately 280 book pages) focuses on dietary questions that the Bible leaves open. Who may act as a slaughterer? What are proper and improper acts of slaughter? What should you do if you find a live fetus in the uterus of a slaughtered animal? Which animals may not be cooked in milk? Because the curdling agent used to make cheese (rennet) comes from the stomach of a calf, is rennet considered a meat product? All these questions are addressed by the Rabbis in the Talmud, in the tractate called *Chullin* (a categorical term that refers to all things of a nonsacred nature).

Some Myths about Dietary Laws

Misconceptions about keeping kosher abound. Kashrut is not, as some people think, a style of food involving bagels or blintzes (crepes). Nevertheless, nonkosher restaurants and caterers sometimes advertise their food as "kosher-style," adding to the confusion.

Food advertised as kosher-style often means dishes that were popular among Eastern European Jews: bagels, blintzes, cholent (a stew of slow-cooked potatoes and meat), and kasha varanishkas (groats and bowtie noodles). But there are many Jews around the world who have never even tasted these foods. To Jews in Morocco, Jewish food is pita and hummus (ground chickpeas) and falafel (fried ground chickpeas). To Jews in India, it would be inconceivable to prepare a holiday dish without curry. "Kosher-style," then, means many things to many people.

Kashrut refers to a dietary system, not a culinary style: the meat has been humanely slaughtered, there is no lard in the baked goods, and the preparation of the food has been properly supervised (as explained previously). Hence, it is increasingly common to find kosher Chinese, Mexican, and Italian restaurants, especially in the major Jewish centers of the world. There is no reason this cannot be. As a result, just as a challah (braided egg loaf used for the Sabbath and holidays) may or may not be kosher, the same can be said of a quesadilla.

Some people cite health benefits as the prime reason for the evolution of kashrut. Hygiene is sometimes still offered as a reason to keep kosher, or as a reason it is no longer necessary to keep kosher. In fact, Maimonides offered hygiene as one of the reasons for the dietary laws. Health benefits may figure in a matrix of reasons to adhere to a kosher diet, but it is a myth to think that hygiene was or could be the principal reason behind the vast system of Jewish dietary laws.

Often, people think that "eating kosher" is required of Orthodox Jews exclusively. But the Conservative movement affirms the importance of a kosher diet as well. Reconstructionist Jews also place a high value on observing kashrut. As advocates of vegetarianism, many who embrace the Jewish Renewal movement (a movement founded by Rabbi Zalman Schachter-Shalomi and defined by the nexus of traditional Judaism and the philosophy of Eastern religions such as Zen Buddhism) are likely to follow a kosher diet. And Reform Jews, who in previous generations had spurned kashrut as being irrational and therefore unnecessary, are once again discussing the importance of kashrut, and many are "eating kosher" again. That would make the founder of American Reform Judaism, Rabbi Isaac Mayer Wise, quite happy. He was passionate about the observance of kashrut.

One of the greatest misconceptions that people have about a kosher diet is that all aspects of it are relevant only for Jews. Actually, the first dietary law in the Bible (the prohibition against eating blood) applies to all humankind, not just to Jews. Eating the limb of a living animal is outlawed for all humanity, and is counted as one of the universal Noahide laws, seven universal laws derived from the Bible and considered to be incumbent on all humans, regardless of their faith. Likewise, Adam and Eve, the parents of all peoples, were encouraged to sustain themselves with nothing more than fruits and vegetables.

The first dietary restriction intended specifically for the Israelites is described in the story of Jacob. An angel wrestles with Jacob all night—dislocating his thigh at the hip socket—changes Jacob's name to Israel, and blesses him before departing. "Therefore the Israelites do not eat the sinew that is on the socket of the thigh until this day, for the angel had touched the socket of Jacob's thigh at the sinew" (Genesis 32:33). This particular aspect of the dietary laws is so odd that it attracts attention. It is how the Jews of China came to be known to their fellow citizens as followers of the *Tiao Jin Jao,* the "Sinew-Plucking Religion."

EATING AS A SPIRITUAL METAPHOR

The Jewish dietary practices, then, are not ends in themselves. They are part of a pattern of living in which following one commandment leads to following another—a system whose ultimate goal is to infuse life with a sense of holiness, a reverence for all living things. With kashrut, Rabbi Samuel Dresner writes, "Judaism takes something which is common and ordinary, which is everyday and prosaic, and ennobles it, raising it to unexpected heights, informing it with profound significance by laws of *what* to eat and *how* to eat, by teaching that every act of life can be hallowed, even the act of eating. Rabbi Abraham Joshua Heschel gave classic expression to this thought when he wrote that 'perhaps the essential message of Judaism is that in doing the finite, we can perceive the infinite.'"[4]

CHRISTIAN PARALLELS TO KASHRUT

Much has been written about the Christian view of the kosher dietary laws. The Gospel of Mark includes a famous statement by Jesus that what defiles a person is not what goes in the mouth but what comes out: "evil thoughts, fornication, theft, murder, adultery, coveting, wickedness, deceit, licentiousness, envy, slander, pride, foolishness" (Mark 7:14–23). In this statement Jesus is not necessarily overturning the dietary laws. Rather, he is establishing the primacy of moral deeds over religious purity alone. In a side comment, the Gospel writer tells us, "Thus he declared all foods clean" (Mark 7:19). Many New Testament scholars contend that this statement is more reflective of Mark's agenda to distance the church from Judaism than it is of Jesus's own attitudes. Presumably, as an observant Jew, Jesus maintained a kosher diet.[5]

In refraining from eating pork, Seventh-Day Adventists practice dietary laws bearing some relevance to kashrut. Some Orthodox Christian practices resemble other aspects of kashrut. For example, certain Orthodox Christians are prohibited from eating meats that come from animals that were strangled, as opposed to ritually slaughtered. This means that, instead of slitting the throat and letting the blood drain out, the butcher strangled the animal, keeping the blood in the system of the animal while it is prepared to be sold. The canons of the church say that a hunter must slit the throat of his kill and let the meat hang upside down for the blood to drain. Similarly, the Ethiopian Orthodox Church instructs its adherents to follow the dietary restrictions set forth in the Hebrew Scriptures.

When the Catholic Church no longer forbid meat-eating on Fridays (this prohibition was lifted in 1966), some

Christians embraced the daily spiritual discipline implied by kashrut as a substitute for the weekly practice of forgoing meat. Christian writer Garret Keizer advocates this discipline: "Two or three dietary restrictions prayerfully chosen, freely embraced and widely observed, two or three refusals as simple and quiet as a child's table grace, and the world would stand amazed. Behold, the kingdom of God remains in that place where Jesus put it on the night in which he was betrayed—in fact, where most of the other things we lose sight of are bound to turn up—right on the kitchen table."[6]

3

PUTTING ON TEFILLIN (PRAYER BOXES)

Bind them as a sign on your hand and let them serve as a symbol on your forehead.

—DEUTERONOMY 6:8

THE BASICS OF USING TEFILLIN

PHYLACTERIES. Black leather boxes. Laying tefillin. Wrapping the straps. These are words and phrases that refer to the admittedly peculiar Jewish practice of literally binding ourselves with the word of God by wrapping a black leather strap—attached to a specially made matching leather prayer box—around the arm and hand. A separate strap with a slightly larger box is wrapped around the forehead—straps left dangling on the side, draped around the neck, hanging down in front. This is what is referred to by the general term *tefillin* (ti-FIL-lin), a plural Hebrew word that emerges from the root word for prayer, *tefillah*. In these boxes are contained essential Jewish prayer texts, taken from the Torah, teachings that *bind* us to God. Putting on tefillin is a ritual act that reflects faithfulness and is based in biblical instruction. In addressing the ancient Israelites, this is the way that the Bible frames it:

Pay attention, Israel! Adonai is our God, Adonai alone. You should love Adonai your God with all your heart, with all your soul, and with all your substance. Take to heart these instructions with which I charge you this day. Impress them on your children. Recite them when you stay at home and when you are away, when you lie down and when you get up. Bind them as a sign on your hand and let them serve as a symbol on your forehead, inscribe them on the doorposts of your house and on your gates.

—DEUTERONOMY 6:4–9

The preceding text from Deuteronomy, one of the four texts written on parchment and actually encased in the tefillin, is from the creedal prayer called the *Shema,* which contains within it the commandment to wear tefillin. The Rabbis of the Talmud maintain that if you say the *Shema* without wearing tefillin, you are a liar. Since the *Shema* prayer includes the commandment for tefillin and the essence of wearing tefillin and saying the *Shema* is the same—to recognize God's power—if you did one without the other, you would be inconsistent, and thus a liar.

FOLLOWING GOD'S INSTRUCTIONS FOR YOUR LIFE

Another of the four texts contained in the tefillin is the second paragraph of the *Shema* prayer. These verses do not use the word tefillin; rather, they literally say to wear "symbols" between the eyes. Jewish tradition has always taken the Hebrew word for "symbols," *totafot,* as referring to tefillin. But Jewish practice is to wear the tefillin on the forehead and not exactly between the eyes, as the Bible suggests. The Rabbis of the Talmud explore this point in depth and conclude that between the eyes is too small an area; therefore, the Scriptures must mean the place where you can make a bald spot, that is, the forehead:

If you obey the instructions that I give you today, loving Adonai your God and serving God with all your heart and soul, I will grant the rain for your land in season, the early rain and the late. You will gather in your new grain, wine, and oil—I will also provide grass in the fields for your cattle. Thus, you will eat your fill. Take care not to be lured away to serve other gods and bow to them. For God's anger will flare up against you, and God will shut up the skies so that there will be no rain and the ground will not yield its produce; and you will soon perish from the good land that God is assigning to you. Therefore impress my words on your very heart; bind them as a sign on your hand and let them serve as a symbol on your forehead, and teach them to your children—reciting them when you stay at home and when you are away, when you lie down and when you get up; and inscribe them on the doorposts of your house and on your gates—to the end that you and your children may endure, in the land that Adonai promised to your ancestors to assign to them, as long as there is a heaven over the earth.

—DEUTERONOMY 11:13–21

The practice of putting on tefillin is a concrete response to the instruction from the Bible to "bind them as a sign upon your hand and let them serve as a symbol on your forehead." Wearing tefillin is a reminder of our responsibilities to God in appreciation for setting us free from Egyptian slavery. Tefillin are wrapped around the arm to remind us of God's "outstretched arm" and God's "mighty hand"—phrases in the Bible that describe God saving Israel from the Egyptians. By recalling God's power in saving ancient Israel from Egypt, we daily remind ourselves of God's power to save us from spiritual and physical enslavement.

By literally binding God's word to the arms, we give unique physical expression to the abstract notion of inviting the Divine into our life for inspiration and guidance. Laying tefillin (a Yiddish expression for putting them on) is the way practicing Jews begin each day; it is part of the morning prayers and serves as a foundation for the hours that follow.

MY OWN EXPERIENCE

While the practice of putting on tefillin has been part of the (solely) male Jewish experience for many generations, tefillin were not a constant part of my own life. My traditional grandfathers used them daily—they were even buried with them. My own father used tefillin as a young adult, but I have no recollection of ever seeing him put them on.

My own daily spiritual practices grew as I passed into adulthood, but tefillin remained foreign to me. Nonetheless, I purchased for each of my sons a pair of tefillin for their bar mitzvah (a Jewish rite of passage for thirteen-year-old boys), gifts brought back from annual trips to Israel. I wanted them to have this ritual opportunity that had passed me by in my youth. Something deeply embedded in my soul yearned for expression through tefillin, though I did not know how to articulate it and did not realize that I could give it voice by simply putting them on. Instead, like so many other things we do as parents, I tried to express myself vicariously through my children.

And then my boys, prompted by their involvement in our local synagogue youth group and the conventions and trips in which they participated, started getting up early each day to put on tefillin before going to school. There was no internal debate, no one there to question their motives or practice. Sleepily, they would wake early and lovingly wrap these leather straps around their young and innocent arms and heads as inoculation against the world's callousness. I pretended to pass their rooms each morning for different reasons, but the real reason remained the same: I was taken by the expression on their faces that accompanied their daily practice. Tefillin helped center the roller-coaster ride of adolescence that they endured each day. "Perhaps it might help center me as well," I thought. So, one morning, I added the practice of tefillin to my daily morning routine.

It was awkward at first. I knew the rules and the how-to of the wrapping technique. I knew the laws and the texts. But they had become somewhat irrelevant. I knew that routines take time to develop and I had to work out my own. Like new physical exercises that are peculiar at first, the fluidity of this practice was slow in coming, so I worked at it each day, carefully binding myself in the leather straps and prayer boxes, concentrating and focusing, avoiding the distractions of the emerging day. In some ways, these first days of laying tefillin were among the most honest ritual practices in which I have ever engaged. The practice of tefillin demanded my attention, for it did not come naturally or easily. I could not multitask as I did it or do it half-heartedly. After all, I was attempting to make contact with God.

After my morning prayers are finished and I remove the tefillin, telltale signs of the practice are left behind—reddened skin indentations on the arm and forehead, and a messy head of hair. But these are not disconcerting. Rather, I find these signs comforting as I look in the mirror and finish the process of readying myself for the day. I am proud of these marks, and I sometimes look for them on others as I encounter them on my way to work. This may remind Christians of the feeling they have following an Ash Wednesday service, when they have ash on their foreheads and wonder "Should I wash it off, or am I supposed to leave it there all day?" In a similarly physical way, through my tefillin practice I remind myself daily of God's presence in my life, the nearness of the Divine, and the inspiration and guidance that I constantly seek.

Each morning I get up, get mostly dressed, and put on my tallit (prayer shawl) and tefillin before finishing my morning routine and rushing off to work. Sometimes I get up a little earlier, stow my tallit and tefillin in my briefcase, and make a stop at a neighborhood synagogue or one near my office for morning prayers. I also keep a set of tefillin in my office, which is particularly helpful in winter, when I often get to my office before the sun is up. As personal as the practice of tefillin is for me, I often yearn for a greater sense of community. I feel better when I join with others in a practice that makes me feel like a disciplined Jew. And I get particular joy from helping a new person who has joined us, awkwardly struggling with the practice, not wanting to ask for help or appear unsure about what to do.

So I gain a significant measure of spiritual fulfillment through my discipline. In an odd sort of way, it is a feeling similar to the one I get after forcing myself on the treadmill each evening, knowing how much better I will feel at the end of my workout, even if I dream up lots of excuses not to do it in the first place.

—KO

THE BASICS OF USING TEFILLIN EACH DAY

Tefillin are worn each morning (except on the Sabbath and holidays) and during the afternoon on Tisha B'Av (a summer holiday commemorating the destruction of the ancient Temples). With a special formula of blessing, they are usually put on at the very beginning of the morning prayer service and kept on through its conclusion. First comes a meditation to help us get spiritually focused on the task. Some use words that spring from their hearts. Others utter prayers that are included in most prayer books. This is one of my favorites, penned by Rabbi Rami Shapiro:

> I welcome this morning in peace; opening my heart to wonder and feeling the presence of God around and within me. I reach out and connect with all those who lift their souls in prayer, adding my voice to theirs in a choir of peace and healing.

Then the arm is placed through the loop of the tefillin. We pause and say a blessing before wrapping the arm:

> *Barukh ata Adonai Elohenu Melekh ha-olam asher kidshanu bemitzvotav vetzivanu lehaniach tefillin.*
> Praised are You, Adonai our God, Sovereign of the universe, who has made us holy with *mitzvot* and instructed us to wrap tefillin.

We temporarily wrap the remaining length of strap around the hand and pause so that we can place the head *tefillah* (singular) where it belongs, on the forehead. We pause once again for a second blessing, much like the first, followed by a statement of affirmation:

> *Barukh ata Adonai Elohenu Melekh ha-olam asher kidshanu bemitzvotav vetzivanu al mitzvat tefillin.*
> Praised are You, Adonai our God, Sovereign of the universe, who has made us holy with *mitzvot* and instructed us concerning the mitzvah of tefillin.

Barukh Shem kavod malchuto l'olam vaed.
Praised is God's name whose sovereignty endures forever.

Then as we unwrap the loosely wrapped hand and wrap it again in a particular way around the fingers and hand, we recite words from the prophet Hosea:

Ve'ayrastikh lee l'olam ve'ayrastikh lee betzedek u'mishpat u'vchesed u'vrachamim ve'ayrastikh lee be'emunah veyda'at et Adonai.
I will betroth you to Me forever. I will betroth you to Me with righteousness, with justice, with kindness and with compassion. I will betroth you to Me with faithfulness, and you shall know God.

—HOSEA 2:21–22

It is one complete sequence of rituals, done without interruption.

Tefillin are wrapped around your weaker arm. Therefore, right-handed people wrap them around the left arm, and left-handed around the right arm. While the manner in which they are wrapped differs slightly in some communities (for example, some wind clockwise while others wind counter-clockwise), the straps of the tefillin symbolically spell out the letters that form a name of God (*Shaddai*/Almighty; note that *shaddaim* is the Hebrew word for "breasts," emphasizing the nurturing aspect of God).

Each *tefillah* contains four excerpts from the Scriptures, but the order and placement of these biblical texts differs for each one. In the *tefillah* for the arm, all four sections appear together on one piece of specially prepared parchment, written by hand with special ink. On the head *tefillah*, the excerpts are written on four separate pieces of parchment and separated into sections.

CHRISTIAN PRAYER-TOOL PARALLELS

There is one mention in the New Testament of tefillin. In the Gospel of Matthew, Jesus makes a comment about the phylacteries that the Pharisees in the Temple are wearing: "The scribes and the Pharisees sit on Moses's seat; therefore, do whatever they teach you and follow it; but do not do as they do, for they do not practice what they teach.... They do all their deeds to be seen by others; for they make their phylacteries broad and their fringes long" (Matthew 23:2–3, 5). The comment seems to reflect contempt for those who wear tefillin as an outward sign of piety but who are far from pious in their actions. Interestingly, some scholars do not read this as a rejection of the ritual practice of tefillin. On the contrary, they see this as Jesus literally telling his followers that their tefillin should not be as broad as the Pharisees'. If Jesus himself donned tefillin (a distinct possibility), then the two traditions might have been much closer in practice had the early church sought to emphasize its ties with Judaism rather than playing up its differences.

Christian tradition does not have a close parallel for the donning of tefillin, although the physicality of the tefillin may remind some of the rosary beads that Catholics use for prayer. Traced back to the ninth century, the rosary is used by Roman Catholics and Anglicans to focus their prayers or meditations.

At a deeper level, what the rosary and the tefillin have in common is the desire for a tactile sensation of prayer. Both of these rituals allow you to literally feel prayer in your hands and on your body. This physicality may be a natural impulse for people who pray regularly. Both of these rituals allow the body to pray, as it were, with the mind and the soul.

4

WRAPPING THE TALLIT (PRAYER SHAWL)*

Speak to the Israelites and tell them they should make
fringes on the corners of their garments for generations;
they should place a twisted thread of blue on the corner
fringes.... When you see it, you will remember all of the
instructions of God and you will do them. You will not
follow after your heart and after your eyes by which you
are seduced. Thus you shall be reminded to do all My
commandments and be holy to your God.

—NUMBERS 15:38–40

THE BASICS OF WEARING A TALLIT

IN ONE SIMPLE, straightforward statement, the Bible makes clear
its instruction to wear a garment with fringes on it: "You shall
make for yourself fringes *(tzitzit)* on the four corners of your
clothing with which you cover yourself" (Deuteronomy 22:12).
The fulfillment of this commandment to wear *tzitzit* (fringes)
takes the form today of a small, four-cornered, fringed garment
(called a *tallit katan,* "small tallit") worn under one's clothing;
and a specially designed shawl (called a *tallit gadol,* "large tallit")
worn over one's clothing during morning prayers. The *tallit*

---

* Some of the material in this chapter is based on "Tallit and *Tallit Katan*" by Haviva
Ner-David in *The Rituals and Practices of a Jewish Life: A Handbook for Personal
Spiritual Renewal.*

katan is the less well known of the two forms because it is worn, for the most part, only by Orthodox men. It is put on in the morning and worn all day. While it is generally worn under other clothes, some let the *tzitzit* of the *tallit katan* hang out from underneath whatever they are wearing. Others choose to wear it over their other clothes as an outer garment.

The *tallit gadol,* generally referred to simply as a tallit, is worn by Jews of all movements every day during morning prayers. On only one occasion of the year is the *tallit gadol* worn at night—on Yom Kippur (the Day of Atonement), the most sacred holiday of Judaism. Normally the *tallit gadol* is wrapped around the shoulders, but some people cover their heads with the tallit during the recitation of the *Amidah* prayer (which forms the core of each prayer service). This allows us to withdraw from the congregation in personal prayer even as we are in the midst of others. The tallit is commonly worn by the service leader during afternoon and evening services as well.

WHY WEAR A TALLIT?

We wear the tallit to constantly remind ourselves to stay away from sin, and to aspire to holiness at all times. This first aspect—the avoidance of sin—is seen in a colorful talmudic story (*Menachot* 44b) about a man who desires to sleep with a prostitute, known throughout the land for her beauty and wealth. Before he goes ahead with this plan, though, the fringes of his tallit miraculously rise up and slap him in the face to remind him that he is straying from the right path. Upon seeing the man's piety and self-control, the prostitute recognizes the error of her ways, repents, and marries him.

Christian readers may be surprised to learn that a story in the writings of the Rabbis concerns visiting a prostitute, but the Talmud is quite explicit about the necessary role of sexuality in our lives. This story is, however, more about piety than sex. It is admittedly fanciful, but its hyperbole spotlights the power of the tallit: it slaps us on the face as a constant reminder to stay on the proper moral path.

The other aspect of the tallit—to remind us to aspire to holiness—is woven into the material of the tallit itself. The Rabbis of the Talmud tell us that the fringes of the tallit are made of a blend of linen and wool, a combination that the Bible prohibits (Deuteronomy 22:11). You would, of course, presume that the tallit would be made from anything *but* a prohibited material. But the Rabbis understood that garments of linen and wool were prohibited because the priests in the holy Temple wore this mix of material and it would be presumptuous to wear priestly garb. However, the Rabbis decreed that we are allowed to wear a small symbol of priestly clothing, to remind all of Israel to strive for the level of holiness associated with the priesthood.

By putting on *tzitzit* (also called *tallit katan*) each morning, we perform a concrete ritual to remind us throughout the day of our personal covenant with God. In a very intimate way, we renew this covenant each morning afresh. The practice of donning a tallit may remind some Christians of the cross worn on a chain around the neck or, for young people, the *WWJD?* bracelets.

The *tallit katan* that is worn under clothing also reminds us of the holiness of the body. When the Bible says that each person is created in the image of God, this does not mean that God looks like a human being. It means that our bodies and spirits are holy. By wearing a holy garment next to our skin, we are reminded of this profound notion, and we can feel, in a very physical way, that we are created in the image of God.

There is another rationale for wearing a tallit that comes from Jewish mystical sources. Rabbi Yehuda Leib Alter of Ger, a nineteenth-century leader in the Hasidic tradition (a revolutionary movement within Judaism that originated in Eastern Europe in the eighteenth century), says that we wrap ourselves in a tallit "to unite with the root of Oneness." The four corners of the tallit, according to the Rabbi of Ger, are symbolic of the four corners of the universe, and wearing the tallit symbolizes bringing together the corners of the world into one place and one being. This gathering together of separate things is a form of unification, an act of oneness connecting us, as wearers of the tallit, with the Oneness at the root of our soul.

Moving from the symbolic to a more practical level, the *tallit gadol* that is worn during morning prayers can also enhance the focused, meditative concentration in prayer, what is called *kavannah* (literally, "direction," as in turning your thoughts in the direction of heaven during prayer). By simply pulling the *tallit gadol* over the head, a person at prayer can block out the world's distractions. We can be in a synagogue full of people or at home while family members rush around in the morning to get ready for school and work, yet by donning a *tallit gadol,* we feel that we are standing alone before God.

HOW THE *TZITZIT* ARE USED DURING PRAYER AND AT OTHER TIMES

The *tzitzit* are used at various times during a service. Just before reciting the *Shema* prayer, those at prayer gather together the four *tzitziot* (plural of *tzitzit*) and hold them, using them to cover the eyes during the recitation. Some people suggest that this symbolically helps worshipers focus on the unity of God, and gives them a special awareness that helps them to concentrate on the words of the prayer. It is customary to kiss the *tzitzit* during the recitation of Numbers 15:37–41, when the word *tzitzit* is mentioned as part of the *Shema* prayer.

Jewish people also use the *tzitzit* as a way of kissing the Torah during its procession around the synagogue before and after its reading. It is also a custom to take the *tzitzit* and lift them toward the Torah when it is raised following its public reading. When called up for a Torah honor (the blessing before and after the Torah reading), it is customary to take the fringes and touch the section of the scroll about to be read, kiss the *tzitzit,* and then recite the blessing before the reading. This procedure is repeated following the reading and before the second blessing.

Traditionally, men are buried in their tallit with a *tzitzit* cut to make it ritually unfit, since one should not bury a ritual object that is still able to be used. The tallit follows you from birth to death; it is often used to wrap a baby during the ritual of *brit milah* (circumcision) or baby naming (for girls), and it is often draped across the casket during a funeral. Although the tallit accompanying a deceased person is no longer fit for use, Rabbi Adin Steinsaltz says that it still offers a kind of divine protection for the perilous journey he or she may face.

The tallit is sometimes used as a *chuppah* (marriage canopy). In addition, it is worn by those carrying the Torah scrolls during the Torah procession in the synagogue prior to and after its reading, as well as on Simchat Torah, the holiday celebrating the completion of the yearly cycle of Torah reading.

WOMEN AND WEARING A TALLIT

In writing an introductory book on Jewish rituals, we run the risk of giving readers the mistaken impression that, because we state things in a direct manner, the issues we address are relatively free from complication. For example, women in liberal synagogues may wear a tallit if they choose, while women in Orthodox synagogues are not allowed to wear a tallit—plain and simple. Well, actually not so simple.

Throughout history, some Orthodox Jewish scholars have argued for allowing women to wear *tallitot* (plural of tallit). The Talmud (*Menachot* 33b) records a debate on this subject between two Rabbis: one permits women to wear a tallit and the other does not. While no one knows who won the debate, we can see that, almost two thousand years ago, some women were doing something that is not permitted today in many circles. In fact, the great medieval Jewish scholar Maimonides wrote in his collection on Jewish law that women may wear *tzitzit* if they so desire (*Hilkhot Tzitzit* 3:9). They are not obligated to do so, as men are, but they are not prohibited from doing so either. Orthodox women today do not wear a tallit because of religious and cultural norms. But because there is some basis in Jewish sources for women wearing a tallit, there may yet come a time in the Orthodox world when this becomes accepted practice.

CHRISTIAN PARALLELS TO WEARING *TZITZIT*

Just as with the wrapping of tefillin, the Gospels suggest that Jesus himself wore *tzitzit* (on a tallit). The Gospel of Mark says that the ill would grab hold of "the fringe of his garment" (Mark 6:56). The word used for "fringe" in this passage, the Greek word *kraspedon,* is also the word used for *tzitzit.*[1] Thus, some scholars infer that Jesus, as a ritually observant Jew, wore *tzitzit.*

Despite this mention in the Gospels, the practice of wearing *tallit katan* did not become a part of early Christian tradition, and remains rather unique to Judaism, since it represents a way of literally wrapping yourself in God's commandments and acknowledging God's constant presence in your life. There are, however, some Christian parallels to the practice: many Christians wear a cross around their neck at all times, affirming their faith in Jesus; others wear the medal of a particular saint as an acknowledgment of God's presence in their life and the values represented in the saint's life; some members of monastic orders wear a scapular under their clothing—a small, woolen cloth that reflects, as the tallit does, a constant commitment to religious values; and some churches, particularly independent apostolic churches, have chosen to use liturgical vestments very similar to the tallit, which are seen as related to the original priestly garb of the ancient Temple in Jerusalem.

Another interesting Christian parallel to the wearing of a tallit comes from the Church of Latter Day Saints (the Mormons). Just as a *tallit katan* is worn under clothing, Mormon tradition holds that followers wear a special garment beneath their clothes. Some speculate that this practice originated because the founder of the Mormon Church studied Hebrew with an observant Jew. Similar to the rabbinic story related previously—about the man whose tallit keeps him from sleeping with a prostitute—there is a Mormon story that says this special garment keeps a man from sleeping with a woman who tries to seduce him, only to eventually marry her after she becomes a pious woman.

5

COVERING THE HEAD

Cover your head so that the fear of God may be upon you.
—*SHABBAT* 156B

THE BASICS OF COVERING THE HEAD

THERE IS PERHAPS no more identifiable outward sign of Jewish identity than wearing a *kipah* (pronounced KEE-pah, also known as a yarmulke in Yiddish or a skullcap in English). Wherever I travel, in Jewish or Christian circles, people generally recognize my *kipah* as a sign that I am a Jew. Interestingly, even though it is such a recognizable symbol of Judaism, nowhere is it prescribed in Jewish law that we must wear a *kipah*. Judaism distinguishes between law and custom. Jewish law refers to rules that are binding on observant Jews; customs are optional observances. Nevertheless, people often adhere to the pressures of community customs more stringently than they do to the demands of law. The wearing of a *kipah* is a custom that developed through the ages, with Jews wearing different types of headcoverings at different times and places. While most Jews who wear a *kipah* are religiously observant, a small number of Jews wear a *kipah* simply out of ethnic pride, to identify themselves publicly as Jews (a practice that may have been adopted following Israel's decisive victory in the 1967 Six-Day War, which created a surge of Jewish ethnic pride). Today, *kipot* (kee-POT, plural of *kipah*) are typically round; some have prayers inscribed on them, some have sports team logos or a fuzzy bear stenciled on them for kids. Most often they come plain and unadorned, reflecting the simple humility that lies at the core of wearing one, reminding the wearer that there is One greater than us. This contrasts with the practice of many Christians, who honor God's presence by taking their hats off in church rather than putting one on.

—DJ

THE BASICS OF OBSERVANCE

Unlike many of the other rituals covered in this book, there is no blessing for wearing a *kipah*. Most Jewish rituals have a traditional blessing that praises God for the opportunity to perform the particular ritual. But the wearing of a *kipah* is a very simple act. We just put it on when we wake up in the morning and that's about it. That is the simplicity implied in the text from Genesis that is often used to justify the practice of wearing headcoverings: "And Jacob went out from Beersheva and traveled toward Haran" (28:10). The Rabbis infer that Jacob would not have left his home with his head uncovered—especially since we know he encountered God on the way, during his dream of a ladder reaching to heaven.

At this time, the custom of wearing a *kipah* is followed predominantly by Orthodox men, who wear it in all places throughout the day. In most non-Orthodox synagogues (Reform, Reconstructionist, and Conservative), you must cover your head when interacting with the Torah in any way, so you put on a headcovering when you have an *aliyah* (a Torah honor, making the blessings before and after the Torah reading), when you read from the Torah, or when you study Torah. Some Jews don a *kipah* when they walk into a synagogue for any reason. In some Reform synagogues, these "requirements" are optional; in others they are not.

There is neither a special way to put on a *kipah,* nor a front or back to a *kipah* (unless there is a logo you want to wear in a special place). Typically, you put on a *kipah* as soon as you wake up, even before putting your feet on the floor. Historically, *kipot* were worn on the crown of the head, but there is no standard way to wear a kipah.

A Brief History of Headcoverings in Judaism

The Rabbis of the Talmud tell us that two types of people routinely covered their heads: married men (who were supposed to cover their heads in the presence of scholars as a sign of respect) and mourners. The Talmud also relates a few stories about people who covered their heads and bodies when studying mystical texts or engaging in mystical prayer. One Rabbi even suggested that God covered God's own "head and body," when sweeping past Moses as he hid in the cleft of the rock on Mount Sinai (Exodus 33:12–23).

The practice of covering the head during prayer did not, however, become a custom for all Jewish men until the thirteenth century in Germany (a very late date by the standards of Jewish history). The rabbis of that period offered the same reason for covering the head as do most rabbis today: *yirat shemayim* (awe of God). The word *yirah* (the root of *yirat*) means "awe," and is central to Jewish life. The ten days that are introduced by Rosh Hashanah (the Jewish New Year) and end with Yom Kippur (the Day of Atonement) are called the *yomim noraim,* "days of awe," from the same root, because on these days we stand in judgment before God.

Yirat shemayim means to be filled with a mix of fear and wonder of God. We recognize that there is a power greater than our own, and this power is reflected in joy, in sorrow, in mountaintop vistas, even in the food we eat for breakfast. We recognize that God is the ultimate source of everything. When we cover our heads, we remind ourselves of this reverence for all God's creations.

Historically, Jewish women covered their heads for different reasons than men. The Rabbis equated hair with sexuality. The Talmud considered women who did not cover their hair promiscuous and subject to divorce by their husbands. Traditional Judaism is concerned with modesty, and uncovered hair is considered too provocative for everyday interactions. As a result, the Rabbis required all women to cover their hair during prayer, and required married women to cover their hair at all times to avoid sexually exciting anyone except their husbands.

Up until the sixteenth century, married Jewish women covered their hair with shawls or scarves. Then, in the sixteenth century, some Jewish women began to cover their hair with wigs, sparking a great deal of legal debate: if married women covered their hair so that they would not be desirable to anyone but their husbands, the wearing of beautiful wigs seemed to undermine the spirit of the law. As a result, many rabbis came out against wigs. The majority of rabbis, however, argued in favor of wigs—perhaps reflecting the desires of their wives—and wigs became accepted in most traditional (that is, Orthodox) communities, and remain so today. Most married Hasidic women take the prohibition against uncovered hair a step further: they shave their heads for their weddings and often wear a long scarf at all times.

Muslim women today engage in a similar practice with the *hijab* (veil). To some, it is a way to express their identity, much as the *kipah* emerged following the Six-Day War in 1967. Most argue that it is a reflection of the teaching in the Qur'an that urges women to cover the head as a sign of modesty (Surah 24, verse 31).

Today, a growing number of women who identify with the liberal movements of Judaism have chosen to adopt head-coverings themselves, but by wearing a *kipah* instead of the traditional scarf or shawl. Some liberal women wear a *kipah* in synagogue, and a small number wear one all the time. A woman who wears a *kipah* all day is making a bold public statement. She risks strange looks and even open disapproval or condemnation from some Orthodox members of the Jewish community.

KIPOT AS SYMBOLS OF COMMUNITY MEMBERSHIP

My grandfather served as the vice president of one of New York City's Orthodox synagogues for thirty-seven years, from the mid-1930s until the 1960s. (He said that he never wanted to be president because his father had never been president of the congregation.) He was strictly observant in nearly every way, attended synagogue regularly, and observed Shabbat. Nevertheless, he never once wore a *kipah* outside the synagogue. Now nearly three-quarters of the people who attend the same synagogue he led wear *kipot* all the time: to work, on dates, or at social gatherings.

In the past thirty years, members of the traditional Jewish community have boldly asserted their identity, taking a stand against acculturation and assimilation. Wearing a *kipah* became part of this shift in attitude, observance, and practice.

While the Orthodox world has reassessed the wearing of *kipot,* the Reform movement has similarly engaged in a long struggle over headcoverings. In the nineteenth century, many Reform synagogues had a strict policy prohibiting the wearing of *kipot,* even by rabbis, because they considered headcoverings old-fashioned, doing nothing to inspire a religious attitude. Some synagogues even put up signs that articulated such a policy. The Reform movement officially went on record in 1885 as disavowing headcoverings, but in recent years there has been a strong resurgence among Reform Jews to wear *kipot* and other ritual items in prayer.

Wearing a *kipah* in Israel may be even more complicated than it is in America. The style of *kipah* you wear often indicates where you live and which political faction claims your loyalty. If you are Orthodox and politically conservative, you are likely to wear a colorful knitted *kipah,* called a *kipah serugah.* If you are a bit more moderate, you generally choose an all-white knitted *kipah.* Students who study in yeshiva (a full-time study center) often wear black felt *kipot.* A suede *kipah* usually indicates that you are an Orthodox from North America and that you consider yourself modern. And wearing a *streiml* (a fur hat with a *kipah* of sorts affixed in its center) means that you are a Hasid, reflecting a tradition that hearkens back to Eastern European *shtetl* (Jewish village) life.

—DJ

THE SPIRITUALITY OF THE HEADCOVERING

By acknowledging the presence of God above, covering the head reminds us that we are in constant dialogue with God, what theologians call a covenantal relationship, one that is not limited to prayer or the study of sacred text; it permeates everything we say and do. As a result, it also has the potential to keep us from straying down the wrong path. When we realize that God is always present, we may think twice about what we say or do beforehand.

CHRISTIAN PARALLELS TO HEADCOVERINGS

Christian women often cover their head in church during prayer—a general sign of submission to God that emerged from 1 Corinthians 11:7–9, which says:

> For a man ought not to have his head veiled, since he is the image and reflection of God; but woman is the reflection of man. Indeed, man was not made from woman, but woman from man. Neither was man created for the sake of woman, but woman for the sake of man.

Some argue that the practice originally represented an acknowledgment by women of their inferiority (hence, men did not cover the head) and was later rejected as a result of this sexism.

Another parallel practice to the wearing of a *kipah* is the traditional headcovering worn by Catholic clergy. The pope and bishops wear a skull cap called a zucchetto that looks like a *kipah*. The pope wears a white zucchetto, while bishops wear red ones. The origin of the zucchetto is unclear; it first appeared in paintings in the thirteenth century. In the sixteenth century it became a custom for all clergy to wear a square cap with three or four ridges, called a biretta, over the zucchetto. Finally, the pope, bishops, and cardinals all wear a white mitre, a large, triangular headcovering. The mitre became part of the papal headgear around the turn of the first millennium. The *Catholic Encyclopedia* rejects any connection between the various headcoverings worn by the pope and the biblical descriptions of headcoverings worn by high priests. Since the wearing of a headcovering is restricted to clergy in both the Roman Catholic and Anglican Churches, while wearing the *kipah* is open to all

Jews, the extent to which these two practices are similar is limited.

At a broader level, though, the underlying rationale for wearing the *kipah*—the observance of *yirat shemayim* (fear and awe of God)—is common to both traditions. Christian liturgy is replete with hymns expressing awe of God. Martin Luther, commenting on the verse from Psalms that says we should "serve the Lord with fear, and exult with trembling" (Psalm 2:11), wrote the following: "Let somebody bring this into harmony for me: exult and fear! My son Hans can do it in relation to me, but I can't do it in relation to God. When I'm writing or doing something else, my Hans sings a little tune for me. If he becomes too noisy and I rebuke him a little for it, he continues to sing but does it more privately and with a certain awe and uneasiness. This is what God wishes: that we be always cheerful, but with reverence."

6

STUDYING TORAH

You should teach them diligently to your children, and should speak of them when you sit in your house, when you walk by the way, when you lie down, and when you get up.

—DEUTERONOMY 6:8

RABBI JAKOB J. PETUCHOWSKI, a prominent theologian from the twentieth century, remarked that Jews study Torah the way a person reads a love letter, eager to squeeze the last drop of meaning from every word. Lovestruck recipients of letters from their beloved ruminate over why specific words were chosen and not others. They yearn to discover the reason behind every detail the letter writer included. Like the lovestruck person, the Jewish student of Torah sees an opportunity in every word and every letter to interpret and analyze the Bible for its deepest meaning.

The close scrutiny of sacred texts is the hallmark of Jewish study. For example, the Bible says that at the end of the creation of the world, "On the seventh day God finished the work that God had been doing, and on the seventh day God rested from all the work that God had done" (Genesis 2:2). At first glance, we might read the text as if it said that God woke up on the seventh day, had some coffee, and finished up a few things that had been left over from work the day before. But a close reading of the text helps us to see that there is an apparent contradiction between the first part of the verse and the second part. Did God work on the seventh day, as it says, "God finished the work that God had been doing," or did God refrain completely from working and rest on the Sabbath, as it says, "and on the seventh day God rested from all the work that God had done"?

Rabbi Solomon ben Isaac, an eleventh-century rabbi from France and perhaps the best-known Jewish biblical commentator, suggests two options for understanding the verse. First, he reasoned, God may have finished working at the precise instant that the sixth day transitioned into the seventh day. Thus, we may say that God finished the work and rested on the seventh day. The second possibility is that God did create something on the seventh day. God created rest, because this is what the world was lacking. So the "work" that God did was to create "not working."

These explanations are profound in their simplicity. On one level, Rashi (as Rabbi Solomon ben Isaac is often called) seeks to resolve the apparent contradiction by explaining that it is really not a contradiction at all: God did not work on the seventh day. Instead, God worked until the exact moment that the sixth day moved into the seventh. On the other hand, he suggests that God actually created rest, and therefore, we are obligated to honor God's creation. Resting on the Sabbath is more than simply the cessation of work. Rather, it should be viewed as a unique gift from God, specifically created for us.

One other aspect of Rashi's commentary is worth noting. He offers two ways of looking at the apparent paradox in the text. This has far-reaching implications. One of the most striking aspects of Jewish Bible study is the absence of any single authoritative interpretation. There is no fundamentalism in Jewish Bible study. No one can point to a given interpretation and say that this and only this is what the Bible means. As we see in Rashi's interpretations, even an individual of his caliber feels free to say that there are different possible interpretations for each verse.

Some well-known interpreters' analyses are given more credence than others' because of their stature, but seldom is there unanimous agreement across Jewish communities and through time as to what a given word of the Bible means. The Rabbis say that the Torah has seventy faces, meaning that there are at least seventy different interpretations for every letter of the Torah. I have heard it said by Christians who embark on a course of Jewish study that it is precisely this lack of dogma, this openness to different understandings of the revealed word, that is the most difficult—and the most interesting—aspect of the Jewish approach to study.

While Jewish study is open to varying, often conflicting, interpretations of the sacred text, most students rely on the major interpreters as a starting point in understanding the Torah. Simply put, most Jews do not study the Bible without at least one commentary alongside them. Often it is the commentary of Rashi. Maybe it is the work of Maimonides. It might be a collection of midrashim—an array of interpretations that take the form of stories about the biblical characters. Whatever classic work it is, Jewish study begins by reading the Bible through the lens of historical interpretation. By understanding the Bible through the interpretation of others, the study of Torah becomes an ongoing conversation through time. In studying the Torah, you enter that historical dialogue and quickly become part of it.

What Is Torah?

The words *studying Torah* are somewhat ambiguous. They refer to studying sacred scripture, but *Torah* can actually mean a few different things. In the narrowest sense, study of the Torah concentrates on the first five books of the Hebrew and Christian Bibles (sometimes called the Five Books of Moses)—Genesis, Exodus, Leviticus, Numbers, and Deuteronomy. There is also a broader meaning of *Torah* that includes the study of later books of the Bible, such as the Prophets and the collection known as Writings (Psalms, Proverbs, Job, Song of Songs, Ruth, Lamentations, Ecclesiastes, Esther, Daniel, Ezra, Nehemiah, 1 Chronicles, and 2 Chronicles). Some use the term *Torah* in an even broader sense, to describe the study of any traditional Jewish text such as the Talmud (the oral law, which reads like a series of academic classroom discussions of the Rabbis).

In this chapter, we use the term *Torah* to refer primarily to the first five books of the Bible. It is important to note that, while Christians often refer to the Hebrew Scriptures as the Old Testament, Jews usually refrain from doing so. That would be tantamount to admitting that a *new* testament superseded it. Further, the Christian ordering of the books of the Old Testament differs markedly from the Jewish order of the same books because of a difference in the process of canonization and a decision as to which books should be included in the canon. For example, the books of the prophets come at the end of the Old Testament, while in the Hebrew Scriptures, the prophets are placed in the middle section.

WHY DO WE STUDY TORAH?

The purpose of studying the Bible is not just to better understand the Bible, but to better understand our own lives. The Torah invites us into its text, and only when we enter its depths are we able to fully absorb its profound spiritual message for our lives. Our interaction with the text is what makes the Torah sacred and alive. We interact with the Torah by identifying with the characters in the text and becoming them. We immerse ourselves in the characters' struggles—those of Abraham and Sarah, Isaac, Jacob, and the others—as they navigate their own spiritual journeys through a developing relationship with the Divine. And at the end of the process, when it is time to suspend our study—if only temporarily—we leave the characters, resurfacing into our own lives. But in this process, we leave a little bit of ourselves in the ongoing story of our people, and the text becomes embedded in our soul.

Here are two different examples of Jewish study that both exemplify the power of this process. The first example draws on a nineteenth-century commentary to explain the verse and give us insight into the text. The second example explores what is called midrash—a uniquely Jewish way to interpret the Bible.

Let Me See Your Face

The following scene is described in Exodus 33:17–23. It is a conversation between Moses and God that occurs after the making of the golden calf. God is angry with the people and threatens to remove the Divine Presence from the Jewish people. Moses ascends Mount Sinai and pleads with God to remain with the people. The text continues:

> And the Lord said to Moses, "I will do this thing that you have asked; for you have truly gained My favor and I have singled you out by name." He [Moses] said, "Oh, let me behold Your Presence!" And God answered, "I will make all My goodness pass before you, and I will proclaim

before you the name Adonai and the grace that I grant and the compassion that I show. But," God continues, "you cannot see My face, for humans may not see My face and live." Then God tells Moses, "See, there is a place near Me. Station yourself on the rock and as My Presence passes by, I will put you in a cleft of the rock and shield you with My hand until I have passed by. Then I will take My hand away and you will see My back; but My face must not be seen."

The Jewish way of studying often begins by raising questions about the text, and there are certainly a lot of questions that emerge from this story: Why would you die from seeing God's face? Why can Moses only see God's back? What does it mean for "God's goodness" to pass before Moses? Why does Moses wish to see God's presence?

This last question seems to be crucial in understanding of the text. Moses has already seen the power of God on Mount Sinai. He has already spent forty days and nights on top of Sinai scribing the Torah. But he still wants more. He desperately wants to see God, to be intimate with God, to know God in a way that no one else ever has. You can almost hear the plaintive longing in Moses's voice. Perhaps the impact of this story is felt so powerfully because we have the same desire to see God.

There is one commentator whose words speak powerfully to Bible readers as they review this passage. Moses Sofer, also known as the Chatam Sofer, was the leader of Hungarian Orthodox Jewry at the turn of the nineteenth century. The Chatam Sofer tries to understand what the Torah means when it refers to God's back. He says, "We are only able to comprehend God's ways and recognize how God works in the world in retrospect. Only then is it possible to fathom even a little of what God does. But at the time the event itself is happening, our understanding is unable to grasp God's doing.... And this is the real meaning of 'You will see My back.'" [It is not referring to God's body but to our perspective on time itself.][1] According to the Chatam Sofer, God is telling Moses that God can only be seen after the fact. God's fingerprints can be seen but never God's fingers. We may be able to see the aftereffects of God, but although we may yearn for it, we can never see God in the moment.

Secret Signs

In another example of Jewish Torah study, we focus on the biblical scene where Jacob intends to marry Rachel, but is tricked into marrying her sister Leah. To explore this scene we utilize midrash. This tool of Jewish commentators seeks to fill in apparent gaps in the biblical text by extending the story. The classic works of midrash were written in the first millennium, but people continue to write midrashim (plural of midrash) today.

In the biblical text, Jacob makes a deal with Rachel's father, Laban, that he will work for Laban for seven years, and at the end of that time, Laban will give Rachel to him as a wife. But Laban tricks Jacob on their wedding night and sends Leah, the elder sister, to the wedding bed instead of Rachel. In the morning, Jacob wakes up and is surprised to see Leah beside him instead of Rachel. Jacob complains to Laban, who replies that it is the practice to marry the older before the younger, and if Jacob wants to marry Rachel he must work another seven years. And Jacob does so.

As we did with the previous text, we begin our study by asking questions. How could it possibly be that Jacob did not know that it was Leah and not Rachel with him in the wedding bed? Further, what were the sisters Rachel and Leah thinking during all of this?

The following midrash gives a partial answer to these questions:

> When Jacob explained to Rachel that he wanted to marry her, he asked her, "Do you wish to marry me?"
>
> "Yes," she answered, "but my father is a swindler, and he will surely manage to cheat you."
>
> "Do not worry. I know how to trick him back!" Jacob said.
>
> "I have an older sister. He will not allow me to get married before her but will give you my sister [Leah] instead of me."
>
> "If so, let us now arrange secret signs by which I shall recognize you." Jacob then instructed Rachel in secret signs so that he would know it was her on their wedding night when she was dressed as a bride.
>
> [When the night of the wedding came] Leah was brought out dressed as a bride. But at that moment, Rachel felt terrible for her sister and did not want her to be shamed. So she instructed her sister in the secret signs, so she could fool Jacob.[2]

As you can see, a midrash is a story that extends the biblical text. It can also be understood as a form of commentary. The first goal of the midrash is to resolve some of the questions in the biblical text, so this midrash claims that Jacob did not see that it was Leah because she used secret signs that he had worked out with Rachel. This still may not be a fully satisfactory explanation. Nevertheless, we find in the midrash a deeper message—an implied relationship between the sisters not mentioned in the biblical text. In the midrash we see that

Rachel knows what her father is going to do and finds a way to foil his plan, but at the last moment she cannot go along with it because of her loyalty to Leah. The midrash brings to the fore the dynamic tension of the moment. Rachel is caught between her desire for her beloved and her loyalty to her family. She longs to be married to Jacob, but she also feels compelled to help her sister.

The midrash gives us a human lens on a biblical story, expressing a classic literary theme: a young person facing the dilemma of sacrificing her own desire in order to keep her family's honor. Another midrash makes Rachel's sacrifice seem even more difficult. In the style of Cyrano de Bergerac, this second midrash says that Rachel hid in the closet on the wedding night. When Jacob spoke to Leah, Rachel answered back. This midrash gives voice to the underlying biblical tension. It also attempts to show us that Rachel's decision of self-sacrifice is a noble one. We are meant to understand the great value she places on family loyalty even in the face of her father's trickery.

The Truth of the Text

One of the most difficult questions for modern readers of the Torah is simply this: Who wrote it? Modern scholarship of the Bible (both Jewish and Christian) suggests that the Torah is an edited or "redacted" compilation of the writings of many different authors. A close look at the biblical text supports this notion. Sections appear to be repetitive, obscure, even self-contradictory. If the Bible came from different sources, these discrepancies would make more sense as editing choices. However, for millennia traditional Judaism has taught that the Bible is not the work of human hands; rather, God revealed the Torah to Moses on Mount Sinai, and Moses simply acted as God's scribe and wrote it down.

For a modern religious reader, navigating between these disparate viewpoints creates tension. We could accept the claim that God gave the Torah exactly as written, but this ignores the work of critical scholars. On the other hand, if we accept the claim that the Bible is the product of several human authors, then the biblical text is reduced from divine revelation to a document of human imagination, not unlike a play by Shakespeare or a Greek epic. However, it is self-defeating to reject the Torah as merely a work of human origins and to assume that apparent paradoxes undermine its value. Perhaps the human authors were working under divine inspiration. Surely those who edited the Torah understood that there were so-called contradictions inherent in the text. Our challenge is to understand why these portions were left in and what their underlying message means to us.

The different Jewish movements have different positions on this issue. Orthodox Judaism treats the Torah as a text given by God through Moses on Mount Sinai. Therefore, from the perspective of Orthodox Judaism, the Torah is entirely the revealed word of God, and all of it is divine truth. Thus, much of the effort of Torah study is devoted to trying to follow the instructions of the Torah and to clarify whatever is unclear.

The Reform movement, on the other hand, does not accept the Torah as a document given by God at a specific time and place. The movement accepts the views of biblical scholars that the Torah is a composite document. Thus, aspects of the Torah have been taken as figurative rather than literal truth by Reform Jews. The founder of the Reform movement in North America, Rabbi Isaac Mayer Wise, considered the Ten Commandments as the only part of the Torah that was, in fact, revealed by God.

Reform Judaism speaks of the Torah as "evolving revela-tion." According to this view, the writing of the Torah was the work of religious geniuses who encountered God and wrote about their experience. Evolving revelation suggests that God is still communicating with us, and the purpose of studying Torah is to discover how God communicated to our forebears so that we might be able to discern God's presence in our own lives.

For the most part, Conservative Judaism follows Orthodoxy, although its scholars apply the scientific method to their study. While the Reconstructionist movement is currently undergoing renewal, its classic position is more akin to the Reform movement in its understanding of the Torah. Reconstructionism does not acknowledge an immanent God; as a result, such a God cannot inspire the direct development of a text. What makes the text so important is that it is the collective history of the folk, the people of Israel—a core concept in Reconstructionist thinking.

TORAH STUDY IN JEWISH LIFE

The laws of Torah study demonstrate how vital it is to Jewish communal life. Each Jewish community is obligated to build a house of study; this is considered even more important than building a synagogue. According to the Talmud, we are permitted to destroy a synagogue if it is necessary to do so in order to build a house of study (*Megillah* 27a). Torah study overrides even the building of the Holy Temple (*Megillah* 16b), and desire to study Torah is a permissible reason for children to ignore their parents' wishes (*Shulchan Arukh, Yoreh Deah* 240:05).

After the Romans destroyed the Temple in 70 C.E., the future of Judaism was tenuous. Rabbi Yochanan ben Zakkai asked the Roman emperor Vespasian for permission to set up an academy for Torah study in Yavneh. The request seemed ludicrous to the Roman, so he agreed. In a prescient way, Rabbi Yochanan understood that the constant study of sacred texts would preserve Judaism more than any buildings or riches (*Gittin* 56b). (While rabbis today share a great deal in common with pastors and priests, their role in the life of their congregation remains different. Rabbis do not see themselves as intercessors. Rather, they are primarily teachers and adjudicators of the law. Even their required role in lifecycle events is limited and primarily informed by the conventions of North American religion.)

Jews have stubbornly continued to study Torah no matter what the circumstances. We study Torah for its own sake. We are not supposed to exploit learning or use it for anything other than trying to understand how to lead righteous lives. But the beauty of studying Torah is that taking the words of Torah to heart leads us to action—positive action that compels us to try to improve the world. Maimonides said that "the study of Torah is equal to all the other commandments because study leads to deed. Therefore study takes precedence over deed" (*Hilkhot Talmud Torah* 3.3).

CHRISTIAN PARALLELS TO STUDYING TORAH

Studying sacred scripture is central to both Christian and Jewish religious life. Although the content of what is studied differs, the way that study is revered in both traditions is similar. This is seen clearly, for example, when comparing Jewish and Christian liturgy.

During every Sabbath (holiday, Monday, and Thursday) morning prayer service, the Torah is carried in a processional around the synagogue. People kiss the Torah as a sign of reverence for it. (In some parts of the Jewish world, worshipers bow to the Torah instead of kissing it.) It is considered a high honor to be called to say a blessing before or after the public reading of the Torah. The Torah is treated the same way you would treat a cherished love letter. Christians have the same relationship to the Gospels—priests kiss the Gospel after reading.

In Roman Catholic and Eastern Orthodox churches, there is often a procession in which the Gospel that contains the day's reading is carried forward and placed on the altar. Sometimes it is carried into the midst of the congregation to be read there. The congregation rises for the reading of the Scripture, which is generally followed by a sermon. This is analogous to the brief lesson that is regularly offered after a Torah reading in Jewish worship services.

7

PRAYING DAILY

May the words of my mouth and the meditations of my
heart be acceptable before You, Adonai, my Rock and my
Redeemer.

—PSALM 19:15

THE PURPOSE OF PRAYER

THE FOLLOWING IS a famous story told by the Baal Shem Tov,
the founder of Hasidic Judaism:

> Imagine a person whose business takes him through
> many streets and across the city's business district all day
> long. As a result, he almost forgets that there is a Maker
> of the world. Only when it is the fixed time for after-
> noon prayers does he remember. He says to himself, "I
> must pray now." Then, from the bottom of his heart,
> along with his prayers, he heaves a deep sigh. He feels
> bad that he has spent his entire day focused on unim-
> portant things. This attitude permeates each of his
> prayers. God holds this man very dear; his prayer pierces
> the heavens.[1]

Prayer helps us, Jews and Christians, make a personal connection to God. It enables us to enter into a sacred relationship

with the Divine and then to nurture that relationship through regular and ongoing dialogue. Prayer provides us with the foundation that makes our spiritual journey possible. Coming to know God through this relationship is probably the most challenging but also the most rewarding part of the journey. Not only does prayer help us grow closer to God but it also helps us face and meet the challenges of daily living. In so doing, prayer gives us a chance to reach beyond ourselves and encounter the Divine.

Why pray? There is an old Jewish adage that should be applied to this subject and perhaps just about every word of this book: for every two Jews you will find three opinions. It would be impossible to specify all the purposes of Jewish prayer. The primary purpose is to fulfill the obligation to serve God that is expressed in Exodus 23:25: "And you shall serve the Lord your God." While this act of service once included the Temple sacrifice, its reference today is primarily prayer. Jewish thinkers throughout the millennia have offered a variety of perspectives. Nonetheless, in this chapter, we will describe some of the basic views on the goals of prayer and how prayer functions in Jewish tradition.

The first view holds that the purpose of Jewish prayer is to assess how well you're doing in God's eyes. This comes from the Hebrew word for prayer itself, *tefillah* (pronounced ti-FEE-la). Grammatically speaking, the word *tefillah* is in the reflexive form, meaning that it refers to something that you do to yourself. Thus, prayer becomes a vehicle for personal assessment, which can take the form of introspection and self-evaluation. Prayer means measuring your thoughts and actions and assessing where you can better yourself and come closer to acting in accordance with God. This takes on heightened meaning around the time of the Jewish High Holidays—Rosh Hashanah and Yom Kippur—when there is a great emphasis on figuring out where you have gone astray over the previous year and repenting for those actions.

Rabbi Abraham Joshua Heschel, considered one of the great rabbis of the twentieth century, holds a completely different view of the goal of Jewish prayer. For Heschel, prayer is not about judging yourself; rather, it is solely about praising God. In an interview Heschel gave before he died, he said, "The primary purpose of prayer [in Jewish tradition] is not to make requests. The primary purpose of prayer is to praise, to sing, to chant. Because the essence of prayer is a song, and man cannot live without a song. Prayer may not save us. But prayer may make us worthy of being saved. Prayer is not requesting. There is a partnership of God and man."[2]

Yet another view of Jewish prayer sees the goal as transcending the gulf between heaven and earth by transcending your ego. This view is central to Hasidic Judaism. In this view, what stands between people and God is the ego—our sense of self—and the goal of prayer is to subsume our consciousness of the self into the universal consciousness of the Divine. Two noted scholars of Hasidism put it this way: "The true goal of the worshiper is to enter the world where 'one may come to transcend time,' where 'distinctions between life and death, land and sea, have lost their meaning.' The worshipper seeks to 'concentrate so fully on prayer that one no longer is aware of the self ... to step outside the body's limits.'"[3]

Another purpose of Jewish prayer comes directly from the Bible: prayer as a means of asking God to fulfill our needs. This may be considered the simplest and most elemental purpose of prayer. The Torah is replete with examples of petitionary prayers to God. For example, Moses petitions God on his sister Miriam's behalf after she has been stricken with leprosy: "Please, God, pray heal her!" (Numbers 12:13). The Torah says that "Isaac pleaded with the Lord on behalf of his wife because she was barren; and the Lord responded to his plea" (Genesis 25:21). Abraham's servant prays to God for the successful completion of his mission, "O Lord, God of my master Abraham, grant me good fortune this day" (Genesis 24:12). Petitionary pleas are central to Jewish prayer. Traditional Jewish belief maintains that God is "One who hearkens to prayer"; that is, God will respond to our appeals. Prayers for healing, good health, wisdom, and safe journeys are all petitionary prayers that figure prominently in Jewish worship. Rabbi Joseph Soleveitchik, the leader of modern Orthodox Judaism for many years, said that prayer was the genuine articulation of our needs, so that we could bring those needs to God's attention and ask for help.

As you can see from this brief overview of the various Jewish views of prayer, some focus on ourselves and our needs; some focus solely on praise and thankfulness to God; and some (such as the prayer said on Yom Kippur, the Jewish Day of Atonement) act as confessions before God. All these views are authentic and mainstream. Many Jews hold these perspectives simultaneously. Nevertheless, while our approach to prayer may be different, our actual prayers—their words and structure—have remained relatively constant for millennia.

THE BASIC STRUCTURE OF A JEWISH SERVICE

The daily ritual of prayer begins with morning prayers called *Shacharit* (pronounced SHA-cha-reet), continues with afternoon prayers called *Mincha* (pronounced MIN-cha), and concludes with evening prayers called *Maariv* (pronounced MA-a-reev). Generally speaking, the liturgies of these services do not change from day to day, with the exception of the Sabbath and holidays, when the liturgy shifts to reflect the mood of the day. Orthodox Jews usually pray three times a day, and Jews from other movements do so as well, to a lesser extent. Services are held in synagogues, but because of the obligation to pray in the afternoon, when most people are at work, many people either pray alone or join with other Jews at their workplace for prayer. A service does not have to be held in a special place to be considered a prayer service (although there are some days of the week—Shabbat, Mondays, and Thursdays—when the Torah is read as part of the service, and Torah scrolls are generally only available in a synagogue).

Rather than reviewing the complete liturgy (a task beyond the scope of this brief introduction to the subject), we will focus on a few basic prayers said in every Jewish worship service. The *Shema* (pronounced sh-MAH) is perhaps the best known. The *Shema* is found in Deuteronomy 6:4: *"Shema Yisrael, Adonai Elohenu, Adonai Echad"* (Hear O Israel, Adonai is our God, Adonai is One). Following the biblical directive to recite it "when you lie down, and when you rise up," the *Shema* is recited in both the morning and evening prayer service. Note that this is a collective prayer, addressed to the entire Jewish people rather than an individual person. At its core, the *Shema* is a statement of faith—that the Jewish people believe and accept one God and one God alone.

Franz Rosenzweig, a German Jewish philosopher of the early twentieth century, saw three themes worked out in the prayer service, using the *Shema* as the cornerstone of this idea. For Rosenzweig, the *Shema* represents revelation, our belief in a God who can respond to prayer and stands outside of nature and history. The prayer before the *Shema* contains a theme of creation, and the prayer after the *Shema* is a prayer of thanksgiving for the redemption from Egyptian slavery. Rosenzweig says these three themes—creation, revelation, and redemption—undergird all of Jewish life. These are not static notions;

we experience them at every moment, and we acknowledge this when we recite the *Shema*. God is continually re-creating the world, God is continually revealing Godself to us, and God is continually redeeming us from the slavery (understood metaphorically) that afflicts us today.

The core of the prayer service is called the *Amidah,* literally "the standing prayer" (because we are obligated to stand for it). The *Amidah* is actually considered the center of the Jewish prayer service, and it consists of nineteen smaller prayers, the bulk of which are petitionary prayers for such things as health, wisdom, and fertile land. On the Sabbath, the *Amidah* changes: The petitionary prayers are omitted and replaced with a prayer of thanksgiving for Shabbat. Jewish tradition understands that on the Sabbath, the day of human and divine rest, we do not petition God for anything. Perhaps the *Amidah* is considered so pivotal precisely because, on all days except the Sabbath, it gives us an opportunity to ask God for help. In doing so, we recognize how much of life is out of our control and how small a part of this vast universe we really are when we ask God for help to ensure our well-being.

On the Sabbath another ritual is added to the prayer service: the reading of Torah. (On Mondays and Thursdays the Torah is also read, but the ritual is most moving on the Sabbath.) The Torah comprises the Five Books of Moses written on a scroll. Precise rules govern how to write the scroll; it must be done by hand, so it takes months—sometimes years— for a scribe to finish writing one Torah. On the morning of the Sabbath, a portion of the Torah is chanted with a special melody, which changes from Jewish community to Jewish community. The portion being read, however, is the same in every Jewish community from New York to Buenos Aires to Tel Aviv. A central calendar established in the Talmud details which Torah portion is read each week.

Because Jewish tradition is grounded so firmly in the Torah and its interpretations, the reading of Torah is considered the highlight of the Saturday morning service. We express our love of Torah, and our reverence for God, by reading a portion of God's words to us. Usually, after a reading of Torah, someone gives a sermon based on that week's Torah portion.

PRAYING IN COMMUNITY

One distinctive aspect of Jewish prayer is the necessity of a quorum to say certain prayers. The chanting of the Torah can only be done with a quorum of ten present. Similarly, the Mourners' Kaddish, a prayer said in memory of those who have died, can only be said in the presence of ten Jewish people. (It must be ten men in the Orthodox Jewish community; it can be ten men and/or women in the other movements of Judaism.) This necessary quorum is called a minyan, although the term is often used to refer to small groups gathered for prayers, regardless of the number.

The minyan is a crucial part of Jewish prayer ritual. If you want to pray Jewishly, you must be part of a community. Imagine that you are a Jewish person who wishes to commemorate the loss of a loved one by saying the traditional Jewish prayer. No matter where you are in the world, you need to find a community of Jews conducting services. The requirement of a minyan is profound precisely because prayer can be such a personal and inward-looking experience. Judaism does not want you to lose yourself in that inwardness. So no matter how important prayer is to you, when you are seeking communion with the Holy One, you must always balance your private prayers with a sense that you are praying in community. There can be no Jewish prayer hermits; prayer—and life—must be done with other people.

HEBREW, THE LANGUAGE OF JEWISH PRAYER

Jewish prayers are generally said in Hebrew. Although worshipers in Reform synagogues do say some of the prayers in
the vernacular (that is, English in the United States), as do a
lesser number of Conservative and Reconstructionist synagogues, by and large you can always expect a hefty dose of
Hebrew in a Jewish prayer service. In American synagogues,
many of the people praying do not know Hebrew fluently;
still, Judaism considers the Hebrew language a touchstone for
Jewish spirituality. Among Jews, Hebrew is called *lashon
kodesh,* the "holy language." Throughout Jewish history, Jews
have spoken other languages, such as Yiddish, in their daily
lives, but Hebrew has always been the vehicle for communicating with the Divine. Jewish mystics believed that the very
shape of the Hebrew letters contain within them secrets for
accessing the Holy.

THE *MECHITZAH* AND A BRIEF WORD ABOUT
WOMEN AND PRAYER

Orthodox Judaism differs from the Conservative and Reform
movements of Judaism in one extremely significant way: the
mechitzah (pronounced meh-CHEE-tza), a partition used in
Orthodox synagogues to separate men and women during
prayer. There are a number of reasons suggested for this separation. Foremost among these reasons is the contention that a
woman's voice is a (sexual) distraction for men during prayer.
The *mechitzah* is also used so that unmarried folk do not feel
left out—we relate to God as individuals, not as spouses or
partners—and to prevent an atmosphere of socializing.

 The actual configuration of the *mechitzah* (i.e., whether
the women sit in back behind a partition, or there is a parti-

tion down the middle) differs from synagogue to synagogue. The issue of separating the sexes during prayer has caused much debate within the Jewish world. Movements other than Orthodox do not separate men and women during prayer.

PRAYER AND MEDITATION

One of the alternative modes of daily prayer that has gained renewed attention in recent years is Jewish meditation. Judaism has a long tradition of meditative techniques, most of which are associated with Kabbalah—Jewish mysticism. Some scholars contend, however, that meditation has historically been part of mainstream Jewish practice. Avram Davis, a leading contemporary practitioner and teacher of Jewish meditation, suggests that the word *tefillah* (prayer) was actually used by the Rabbis of the Talmud to mean both prayer and simple meditation:"When they [the Rabbis] use the term *tefillah,* they can easily be referring to either meditation or prayer or possibly to both. It is both a strength and a weakness of modernity that we feel so sharply the need to differentiate between these transformative tools."[4]

Jewish meditation takes many different forms, and new approaches are constantly being explored. The basic goal of Jewish meditation is to clear your mind by focusing your intention on certain phrases from the prayer service or images from Jewish tradition. This helps you relax. Moreover, and more important, the goal of meditation is *devekut* (pronounced de-vei-KOOT), a "cleaving" to God by quieting the mind and making the ego fade into the background. A Jew who meditates might practice on a daily basis or follow the traditional pattern of morning, afternoon, and evening prayers and meditate three times a day. This is similar to Christian centering prayer, also called contemplation. Such prayer is beyond words and includes an opening of the mind and heart.

Christian Parallels to Jewish Prayer

According to a familiar maxim, Christians can walk into a synagogue and affirm just about everything that is said, because the prayers primarily praise and thank God, but Jews cannot walk into a Christian church and affirm any of what is said, because of the extent that Christian prayers invoke Jesus as Deity. While this may be substantially true, you can still find parallel themes in Jewish and Christian prayer services.

Much of Christian liturgy is based on Jewish models. In both Catholic worship services and traditional Jewish prayer services, there is a particular psalm associated with each day. The extensive use of the Hebrew psalms in Christian liturgy points to the connection between Christian and Jewish liturgy. Even the most widely known Christian prayer, the Lord's Prayer (Matthew 6:9–13), is itself based on Jewish sources—almost every line in the prayer has a parallel in Jewish literature. The beginning invocation, "Our Father who is in heaven," is found in some of the blessings of the *Amidah* as well as in the High Holiday liturgy. Many scholars have also noted the close connection between the Lord's Prayer and the Kaddish prayer, which begins, "May God's great name be hallowed in the world that God created, according to God's will, and may God establish God's Kingdom ... speedily and at a near time." The Lord's Prayer and the Kaddish similarly speak of the coming of a better world under God's providence.

Beyond the particular details, it should be noted that the basic categories of prayer—prayers of petition; prayers of thanksgiving; and prayers of confession, although they are limited in Judaism—are the same in both faiths. This may reflect some universal human traits—there are only so many ways to address God—but it also reflects the Jewish origins of the church. In those aspects of Christian prayer that do not center on Jesus's divinity or his suffering, we see similar language and a similar yearning to reach out to the God of all people.

8

SAYING GRACE AND NINETY-NINE OTHER BLESSINGS THROUGHOUT THE DAY

*Rabbi Andrew Vogel**

For the sake of Adonai, the God of Israel: May the angel Michael be at my right side, and may the angel Gabriel be at my left side. May the angel Uriel be before me, the angel Raphael be behind me, and may the Presence of God be upon my head.

—FROM THE LITURGY, SAID BEFORE RETIRING

FOR THE NIGHT

THE BASICS OF BLESSINGS: EVERY DAY IS THANKSGIVING

THERE IS A WELL-KNOWN SCENE in the musical *Fiddler on the Roof,* when Tevye and the other men of the village are discussing the czar of Russia. Someone suggests that a blessing be said on behalf of the czar. Another asks inquisitively, "Is there a blessing for the czar?" The town's rabbi responds, "In Judaism there is a blessing for everything." He continues, "May the Lord bless and keep the czar … far away from us." Although

---

* Parts of this chapter were based on and inspired by the work of Rabbi Nina Beth Cardin.

no such blessing actually exists, the rabbi in the musical is correct: there is a blessing for *almost* everything in Judaism. There is a blessing for getting up in the morning, for going to sleep, for eating, for seeing wondrous things, for experiencing new things, for the occurrence of good things, for the unfortunate occurrence of bad things, for hearing the news of someone's death, for seeing someone you have not seen in a long time, for going to the bathroom, for studying Torah, for going on a journey, for fulfilling almost any religious commandment, and for just about everything else in life.

In the Talmud, one Rabbi instructs us to recite one hundred blessings throughout the day. His teaching is seen as a way for us to develop a posture of gratitude. Jewish tradition encourages a daily practice of reciting blessings of thanksgiving to God for the goodness in our lives each day.

There are two basic types of blessings: those that respond to awe, and those that seek to stimulate awe within us. Blessings that respond to awe are those said when we see or experience something awe-inspiring, such as the birth of a child: *Barukh ata Adonai Elohenu Melekh ha-olam, ha-tov v'ha-meitiv,* Praised are You, Adonai our God, Sovereign of the universe, who is good, and does good. Blessings that seek to stimulate awe within us are those said over routine things, such as the blessing before eating bread: *Barukh ata Adonai Elohenu Melekh ha-olam, ha-motzi lechem min ha-aretz,* Praised are You, Adonai our God, Sovereign of the universe, who brings forth bread from the earth. The blessings over routine acts keep us mindful of God's role in the everyday aspects of life; otherwise we might be dulled into forgetting about God's part in things as basic as the food we routinely eat. Rabbi Abraham Joshua Heschel tells us that blessings help us "to take notice of the wonder, to regain a sense of the mystery that animates all being."[1]

While the distinction between a blessing and a prayer is often very subtle, blessings are generally short, begin with the formula, "*Barukh ata Adonai Elohenu Melekh ha-olam* ... Praised are You, Adonai our God, Sovereign of the universe ..." and are connected to specific acts or activities. Prayers are usually longer, may contain blessings within them (sometimes a blessing begins or ends a theme that is elaborated in the prayer), and do not require any connection to an act. As mentioned in the previous chapter, prayers are often requests we make of God.

The Origins of Blessing in Jewish Tradition

Although there is some mention of blessings in the Torah, the Rabbis of the Talmud conceptualized the structure and content of blessings. Almost all the basic blessings can be found in the first tractate of the Talmud, appropriately called *Berakhot* (Blessings). In this tractate we read about both types of blessings, those that respond to awe and those that seek to inspire awe. Among those that seek to inspire awe are blessings to be said before eating. As noted in the Talmud, "Rabbi Hanina bar Papa says, 'Anyone who enjoys this world without saying blessing, it is as if that person robbed God'" (*Berakhot* 35a). This seems like an odd thing to say; after all, how can you steal anything from God? According to Rabbi Lawrence Hoffman, professor of liturgy at Hebrew Union College–Jewish Institute of Religion, the Reform movement's rabbinical seminary, the point is that everything belongs to God—all the food, all objects, each of us belongs in some sense to God. One psalm makes this clear, "The earth is the Lord's and the fullness thereof" (Psalm 115:16). We say a blessing before eating to transfer the food from God's ownership to human control. Therefore, the blessing reminds us to be conscious of partaking in something that is in God's realm. The blessing evokes God's awesomeness: The whole earth is full of God's glory.

The other type of blessing—a blessing that responds to awe—is also found in the tractate *Berakhot*. The Talmud records that a blessing must be said after participating in miracles, upon observing shooting stars, for seeing unusual-looking people—any moment that inspires awe is cause for a blessing. Surprisingly, a blessing is even said after hearing tragic news. According to the Talmud, "You say a blessing for evil, similar to that said over good" (*Berakhot* 54a). This is a deep theological statement compressed into one sentence. It reflects the basic belief of monotheism: God is ultimately responsible for our lives. Whenever we discern God's presence, whenever we are filled with awe, either for good or bad, we are obligated to praise God.

BLESSINGS THAT SEEK TO IINSPRIE AWE

Morning Blessings

The Jewish practice of reciting blessings specifically in the morning and the evening originates in the Bible. The passage directly after the *Shema* states: "You shall speak of them ... when you lie down and when you rise up" (Deuteronomy 6:5). The Rabbis interpreted this verse, in part, as a requirement for Jews to recite certain passages of the Bible when getting into bed at night, and to praise God upon waking up in the morning.

The Rabbis of the Talmud expanded on the biblical instruction to recite specific passages from the Bible, including additional blessings, which they crafted. Some of these blessings are lengthy statements of thanks and petition; others are more concise, focused, one-line blessings. Some of these blessings are for acts as basic as placing our feet on firm ground, taking our first steps in the morning, and rubbing the sleep from our eyes. Other blessings express thanks to God for creating us in God's image, for making us as we are, and for allowing us to enjoy our precious freedom.

The form of the morning blessings, in Hebrew *Birkot Ha-shachar* (pronounced bir-KOT ha-SHA-char, literally, "blessings of the dawn"), evolved over several centuries. The morning blessings include a blessing for returning to life after sleep, a blessing for the ability to use the bathroom, a blessing for the soul, a series of blessings extolling God's power, and the creedal *Shema* statement.

As you read through the morning blessings below, take note of the balance between blessings for the soul and blessings for the body: the first and third blessings thank God for the soul and its purity, while the others focus on the physical nature of our beings. The blessings evoke gratitude for both soul and body, calling on us to remain mindful of both aspects of ourselves and implicitly reminding us to care for both aspects of our being.

I give thanks to You, living and present Sovereign, for returning my soul to me with love; great is Your reliability.

Praised are You, Adonai our God, Sovereign of the universe, who has made each human being with wisdom, creating in us openings and cavities. You know full well that if one of them were to be incorrectly closed or opened, it would be impossible for us to exist in Your presence. We thank You, God, who heals all creatures, and performs wonders.

My God, the soul with which You endowed me is pure. You created it. You formed it. You breathed it into me. You preserve it within me. In the future, You will take it from me, and return it to me in the world to come. As long as my soul is within me, I thank You, Adonai my God, God of my ancestors, Ruler of all creatures, Master of all souls. We praise You, Adonai, in whose hands are the souls of all the living, and the spirit of all human beings.

Praised are You, Adonai our God, whose Presence fills the universe, who gives [the rooster] the ability to distinguish between day and night.

Praised are You, Adonai our God, whose Presence fills the universe, who made me a Jew.

Praised are You, Adonai our God, whose Presence fills the universe, who created me in God's image.

Praised are You, Adonai our God, whose Presence fills the universe, who opens the eyes of the blind.

Praised are You, Adonai our God, whose Presence fills the universe, who clothes the naked.

Praised are You, Adonai our God, whose Presence fills the universe, who releases the oppressed.

Praised are You, Adonai our God, whose Presence fills the universe, who straightens those who are bent over.

Praised are You, Adonai our God, whose Presence fills the universe, who makes the earth firm upon the waters.

Praised are You, Adonai our God, whose Presence fills the universe, who takes care of all my daily needs.

Praised are You, Adonai our God, whose Presence fills the universe, who guides our steps.

Praised are You, Adonai our God, whose Presence fills the universe, who girds Israel with strength.

Praised are You, Adonai our God, whose Presence fills the universe, who crowns Israel with glory.

Praised are You, Adonai our God, whose Presence fills the universe, who gives strength to those who are weary.

Praised are You, Adonai our God, whose Presence fills the universe, who removes the sleep from my eyes, and who clears away the slumber from my eyelids.

Hear O Israel, Adonai is our God, Adonai is one.

Evening Blessings

The evening blessings are called *Shema She-al Hamitah* (literally, "the *Shema* [that is recited] on the bed"). These blessings consist of the one line of the *Shema* followed by a blessing asking God to protect us while sleeping. The four archangels—Gabriel, Michael, Uriel, and Raphael—are also invoked for protection during the night. There is no standard version for these evening blessings—some prayer books include pages of psalms and praises for God, while others simply offer a core liturgy.

Here is a basic version of the evening blessings (similar to the one found in many Jewish prayer books). As you read through the blessings, you will notice that God is not praised in the evening as much as in the morning. In the evening, petitions are made to God for protection. We call on God and the angels to guard us on all sides. The evening blessings respond to our primal fear of the night, of the darkness, of our own inability to protect ourselves as we sleep. Out of the anxiety that darkness brings, we call upon God to shelter us in peace.

Hear O Israel, Adonai is our God, Adonai is one.

Lay us down, Adonai our God, with peace, and raise us up to life, You who are Sovereign. Spread over us the shelter of Your peace. Set us straight with Your good counsel before You, and save us for the sake of your name [to protect Your reputation]. Hide us in the cover of Your shadow, for You are our Divine Guardian and Deliverer, and You are a merciful and gracious Ruler. Guard our going and our coming, for life and peace, for all eternity. Spread over us the shelter of Your peace. Praised are You, who spreads a peaceful shelter upon us, and upon all of Your people Israel, and upon Jerusalem.

For the sake of Adonai, the God of Israel: May the angel Michael be at my right side, may the angel Gabriel be at my left side. May the angel Uriel be before me, the angel Raphael be behind me, and may the Presence of God be upon my head.

In the ancient world, nighttime inspired fear, as a time of great vulnerability. The Rabbis taught that sleep was "one-sixtieth of death." In one midrash, they imagined that on the first day of Adam's life, after he had experienced only the beauty of sunshine and light all day, Adam grew afraid, seeing the sun set and disappear for the first time. As darkness approached, Adam feared that he would be enveloped by it; he had trusted all day in God, who had created him, but when the shadows started to fall, he began to lose his faith, afraid he would be abandoned or killed. But, the midrash tells us, God heard Adam's worried cries and protected him, teaching him to cope with darkness by lighting fire.[2]

It is no mere coincidence that the Rabbis who imagined this scene chose Adam as the story's main character, as if to say that fear of nighttime is a universal human experience, shared by all. As children, most of us dreaded the monsters of the night, dark closets, and basements. Perhaps we felt anxious at the prospect of being abandoned, or afraid of the unknown. This fear is not limited to children; on some psychological level all adults are afraid of being deserted, or are uneasy with uncertainty. It is human nature to feel safe and secure in what is known and seen and unchanging, and to feel fear in times of darkness. The ancient authors of the evening blessings sought out God in these moments, asking for God's protection and reaffirming their faith in the face of their fear.

In addition to the *Shema's* unwavering statement of faith, the *hashkiveinu* (pronounced HASH-kee-VEI-noo) prayer (literally, "Cause us to lie down") is recited as part of the bedtime *Shema* ritual. This prayer asks God to "lie us down in peace, and raise us up, O Sovereign, to life." It can be understood first as a prayer seeking assurance that we will be safe during the night until morning, and also as a prayer addressing the ancient Rabbis' fear of dying during sleep. They felt that the mysterious nature of sleep was connected to the mystery of death. Thus, these teachers asked God simply to let us wake up. The words of the prayer may also be read as a petition asking God to revive us in the world to come if we do die during the night. Through their ambiguous word choice in this prayer, the Rabbis connected nighttime with death, and addressed our fears of both through a prayer for peace.

The prayer concludes by asking God to "spread over us a sukkah of peace." A sukkah is a wooden outdoor booth constructed for the week of the fall holiday of Sukkot, a temporary shelter in which Jews are directed to dwell for seven days. But the Rabbis of the midrash imagined that the sukkah in which God sheltered the Israelites as they wandered through the desert was not made of wood but rather of six clouds of glory, which represent God's Divine Presence. When we recite this prayer at bedtime, we ask God to shelter us with the same sukkah as we sleep, to surround and protect us with God's Divine Presence on all sides.

The final section of the nighttime blessings also asks God to surround us with divine protection. It invokes four specific angels by name. (Judaism clearly affirms the presence of angels and their work in the world.) This prayer, which begins with *BeShem Adonai* (literally, "In the name of God"), asks the angels to stand guard in positions around us, with Michael at our right, Gabriel to our left, Uriel in front of us, and Raphael behind us. Why invoke these angels? The archangel Michael, according to the midrash and some later Jewish mystical traditions, is the angel of God who serves as the prime defender of the Jewish people. Gabriel, the second most powerful angel, according to the imaginations of the Rabbis of the midrash, accompanies him in the bedtime prayer and stands at our left side. Asking Michael to be at our right side and Gabriel at our left is like asking the armies of General George S. Patton and General Douglas MacArthur to escort us personally through the night.

Uriel and Raphael are more minor angels in Judaism's "angelology," yet they are chosen for specific reasons. The name Uriel means "light of God"; we ask this angel to shine divine rays before us in the dark of night to keep us safe. Raphael, the angel of healing, is perceived by the Zohar, the major Jewish mystical work, as the one who dominates the morning hours, bringing hope and relief to the sick and suffering. The healing that Raphael brings us is spiritual as well as physical. If we take this prayer literally, God's angels will protect us on all our four sides during the night.

Some see each angel as a metaphor for what all of us need emotionally, physically, and spiritually: strength, courage, insight, and health. Invoking the angels in the prayer helps us acknowledge our own limitations as we consider the day just ended and the night ahead. Many of us do not believe in angelic figures as they have been represented in Western art—as chubby, cherubic babies with wings. Yet many of us do place our faith in a God whose multiple attributes can strengthen us in times of weakness, give us courage in moments of doubt, heal us when we are hurting, and provide light for us in the darkest hours.

Blessings before Eating

Jewish tradition requires different blessings to be said before eating different types of food. The blessings recited before eating food reflect our awareness of divine participation in our well-being. We could have only one blessing to be recited before eating—something such as, "God, thanks for the food"—but such an approach would reduce all food to one common category, something to be consumed by us. It would ignore the variety, diversity, and grandeur of nature. Instead, Judaism offers several specific blessings to be recited before eating: one for bread (which may encompass the others); one for other baked goods; one for vegetables and all foods that grow from the ground; one for fruits and all foods that grow on trees; one for liquids, candies, and other categories not included in the previous ones.

These blessings remind us, the consumers, about the diverse and sensitive environment in which we live. They subtly encourage us to attend to the many needs of the world: if we like the variety of foods we are eating, we need to tend to the earth, to enable it to sustain this abundant produce. In Judaism, blessings before eating express our appreciation for having food as well as our wonder at the majesty of nature and technology and our gratitude for the ideal blending of the two. We are even more acutely aware of this when fruit that was once only available seasonally is now in stores throughout the year. Transportation and refrigeration enable us to eat any kind of food any time of the year. Needing to select the appropriate blessing before we eat helps us remain mindful of the labor, the ingenuity, the efforts, the luxury, and the costs of such diversity and availability.

Here are the blessings before eating:

For bread: Praised are You, Adonai our God,
Sovereign of the universe, who
brings forth bread from the earth.

For other baked goods: Praised are You,
Adonai our God, Sovereign of the universe,
who creates all sorts of grains.

For wine: Praised are You, Adonai our God,
Sovereign of the universe, who
creates the fruit of the vine.

For drinks, candies, and the like: Praised are You,
Adonai our God, Sovereign of the universe,
whose word brings all life into existence.

For fruits and produce from trees: Praised are You,
Adonai our God, Sovereign of the universe,
who creates the fruit of the tree.

For vegetables and produce that grows from the ground:
Praised are You, Adonai our God, Sovereign of the
universe, who creates the fruit of the earth.

Blessings after the Meal

Judaism is one of the few religions that has blessings both
before and after the meal, as if to say that it is not sufficient
to give thanks for the food when you are hungry or needy,
but also when you are sated. If the blessings before the meal
speak of our place in nature and our connection to the land
and to God, the blessings after the meal speak of our place in
history, and our connection specifically to the Land of Israel
and to God.

The *Birkat Hamazon* (Grace after the Meal) is rather long
and can be found in most Jewish prayer books. Its multiple
paragraphs are usually said rapidly in a short time. It may seem
odd for the blessing after a meal to be so long, but this blessing contains a number of important ideas. We give thanks to
God for nourishing us with food, but then we also give thanks
for the Land of Israel, the city of Jerusalem, and then for God's
goodness. Various blessings are added for holidays and other
special occasions such as weddings.

Why is there an emphasis on the Land of Israel in the
blessings after the meal? The Torah says, "You shall eat and you
shall be satisfied, and you shall bless Adonai your God for the
goodly land that God gave you" (Deuteronomy 8:10). Before
the meal, our hunger focuses us on our common human
instincts and sustaining life itself—we are creatures dependent
on the earth; humans in covenant with God eager to satisfy
our earthly, creaturely needs. But with the gift of a satisfying
meal, our attention turns to the purpose of life. We eat to survive, but for what purpose? What meaning do our lives have?

Every time we eat a meal, we are reminded that we belong to a people, to a land, and to God. In the company of friends and family or by ourselves, we declare that nourishment is not just a gift. It is a calling. We may eat alone or in small groups, but we live in community, bound to our history and our future. Every act of eating is an act of communion and rededication to the mission of the Jewish people.

BLESSINGS THAT RESPOND TO MOMENTS OF AWE

One of the most popular fixed blessings is the *Shehecheyanu* (pronounced she-HEH-chee-YAH-noo), a unique, unparalleled blessing about being aware of and delighting in the moment. The blessing says: "Praised are You, Adonai our God, Sovereign of the universe, who has given us life, sustained us, and brought us to this very moment [of joy]." This blessing is said at bar and bat mitzvah ceremonies, commencements, retirements, dedications, and other important milestone events. But it can also be said to sanctify the quiet, extraordinary moments of life: when a child takes a first step, when we cut the tags off our new clothes, when our child gets a driver's license, when parents celebrate their fiftieth anniversary. This is a blessing that awakens us to the moment's splendor.

Birth and Death

Throughout our lives, we hear news of births and deaths, graduations and retirements, weddings and divorces. The Jewish religion helps us to process this news, to place it in the context of the broad stream of life. The Rabbis crafted two different responses to such news in the form of fixed blessings.

Upon hearing the news of a death, Jews are instructed to say: "Praised are You, God, the Judge of truth." When we are angry or confused or lost, this blessing shows us the way. It reminds us of what can and cannot be controlled. It affirms faith at a time when faith seems hard to sustain. It reminds us that we cannot fully understand the mysteries of life. When we place our faith, trust, and hope in a power larger than ourselves, we can relax our fists, release the urge to control, and let go of the drive to fix everything—an ability we never had anyway.

Likewise, upon hearing good news, we are told to say, "Praised are You, Adonai our God, Sovereign of the universe, the One who is good and who brings goodness." These words place individual feelings of gratitude in a greater context. In the context of Jewish community, we neither mourn alone nor rejoice alone. These blessings, crafted by the Jewish tradition, remind us as individuals that others care about our feelings, and how we should respond to them. But they also remind us that others celebrate and hurt—that our experiences, while unique to us, are not unique to humanity. None of us is alone in the particularity of our feelings. To recite these blessings helps us to remember who we are and *whose* we are.

Friendship

There is a remarkable blessing in the Jewish tradition that reminds us of how precious constant contact with our friends is. If we do not see or communicate with a friend for over thirty days, Jewish tradition calls on us to greet that friend the next time we see him or her with this blessing, "Praised are You, Adonai our God, Sovereign of the universe, who brings the dead back to life." The Rabbis believed that when we lose touch with a friend, we lose a little bit of ourselves, too. To renew contact is to renew more than the relationship: it is to reawaken the part of us that no one but our friend animates. For each friend enlivens a specific constellation of our spiritual impulses, our desires, our strengths, our hopes, and our memories. Dormant relationships are not necessarily endangered, but they cannot grow, and neither can that part of us that the friendship evokes. Reciting this blessing reminds both friends how long it has been between visits, how valued is their time together, and what a loss it is to be out of touch.

Miracles of Time and Place

Just as we can reconnect with a person, Jewish tradition recognizes that we can reconnect with a place. Places stimulate memories that arouse feelings. That is why, for example, we celebrate anniversaries at the place we first met our loved one, or where we got engaged. Some of us have experienced the miracle of being rescued. Perhaps someone inexplicably appeared to help you in a moment of danger. Or perhaps it was not mysterious, but just as miraculous; for example, a physician removing a diseased organ, replacing a weakened valve, or saving you from infection. Jewish tradition encourages us to mark that place where an act of rescue happened, so when we come upon it again we recite: "Praised are You, Adonai our God, Sovereign of the universe, who caused a miracle to happen here to me."

A Blessing for Everything, Including the Czar

Judaism has a surprising variety of blessings for all types of experiences. Some of them are quite beautiful:

> *Upon seeing something of extraordinary beauty:* Praised are
> You, Adonai our God, Sovereign of the universe,
> who has placed such beauty in Your world.

Upon seeing lightning: Praised are You, Adonai our God,
Sovereign of the universe, who does the
work of creation.

Upon hearing thunder: Praised are You, Adonai our God,
Sovereign of the universe, whose power and might fill
the whole world.

Upon seeing the ocean: Praised are You, Adonai our God,
Sovereign of the universe, who made the great sea.

*In conversation, upon independently awakening to an insight
that reflects one from a sage or colleague:* Praised are You,
Adonai our God, Sovereign of the universe, for enabling
me to share in the wisdom of sages.

*Upon seeing someone distinguished in worldly knowledge, dis-
covery, or invention:* Praised are You, Adonai our God,
Sovereign of the universe, who has given of Your wisdom to those who are flesh and blood.

Health and Recovery

Between life and death are moments of illness or accident. The
Mi Sheberakh (pronounced MEE she-BEI-rach), the classic
prayer for health, is recited in synagogue in front of the Torah
scroll on behalf of a loved one, in the presence of a prayer quorum (minyan). But that is not the only opportunity we have
to recite personal petitions for health. The *Amidah* (the central
prayer of every fixed Jewish prayer service, said three times a
day with or without a congregation) includes a general prayer
for healing: "Heal us, God, and we will be healed; save us and
we will be saved." Jewish tradition also encourages us to add a
personal petition for the recovery of a loved one in the midst
of this statutory prayer: "May it be Your will, God, that You

quickly send a full recovery from Your domain in the heavens to _____ here. May it be a healing of body and a healing of spirit, for them, and all Israel who suffer." You can recite this petition any time of day or night.

A Prayer for Traveling

Knowing how unsettled we and our loved ones can be at the prospect of a long-distance journey, Jewish tradition offers words of comfort to say when leaving home. While crafted for the traveler, these words can ease the way for the traveler and the homebound alike.

The traditional traveler's prayer *(tefilat ha-derekh,* "prayer of the way") reads as follows:

> May it be Your will, our God and God of our ancestors, that You lead us toward peace, and place our footsteps on the path of peace, and guide us toward peace.
> Bring us to our desired destination in life, joy, and peace. Save us from the hand of all our enemies, from ambush, robbers, and evil animals along the way, and from all types of harm that come to the world. Send blessings to all the work of our hands, and grant us grace, kindness, and mercy in Your eyes and in the eyes of all who see us. Hearken to the sound of our supplications, because You are God who hears prayers and supplications. Praised are You who hearkens to prayer.

An alternative text:

> May it be Your will, our God and God of our ancestors, that You lead us away in peace, guiding and direct-

ing our journey in peace. Bring us to our desired
destination in health, joy, and peace. Keep us from
all the harm and misfortunes that roam this world.
Bless our work. Let us find kindness and openness
in those we encounter wherever we go, and before
You as well. Hear our prayer, God, for You are the
one who listens to prayers. Praised are You, the
One who hears prayers.

CHRISTIAN PARALLELS TO JEWISH BLESSINGS

While Christianity does not place the same emphasis on saying prescribed blessings as Judaism does, there are still some
similar traditions. For example, both faiths mandate a blessing
before eating. According to Dr. Lawrence A. Hoffman, editor
of the *My People's Prayer Book: Traditional Prayers, Modern
Commentaries* series (Jewish Lights), Christian and Jewish
blessings recited before eating have an affinity that goes
beyond the mere fact that they both mention *bread*. The
Lord's Prayer includes the plea, "Give us this day our daily
bread." Church leaders said that this refers not to ordinary
bread but rather bread of the Kingdom. That is, bread of the
world to come, when the world will be redeemed. Similarly,
the Talmud says that the bread mentioned in the Jewish blessing, "Blessed are You ... who brings forth bread from the
earth," is not just ordinary bread. Rather, it is the bread from
the world to come when God will really bring forth bread.
Interestingly, both the church leaders and the Rabbis of the
Talmud see the blessings said before eating as a portent of
future redemption.[3]

At a broader level, Judaism and Christianity share a basic
outlook of thanksgiving. Both traditions view God as the
Creator of all, and thus understand that we must thank the

root of creation for everything we receive, the blessings in our lives. While the forms of thanksgiving differ between the two religions, the essence of why Christians and Jews say blessings at all is the same: thankfulness brings us closer to the Holy One.

9

GOING TO THE RITUAL BATH

Debra Nussbaum Cohen

So he [Naaman] went down and immersed himself in the
Jordan seven times, as the man of God had bidden; and
his flesh became like a little boy's, and he was clean.
—2 KINGS 5:14

THE BASICS OF SPIRITUAL BATHING IN JUDAISM

AS PART OF a large set of laws involving "family purity," the
sacred commandment of *mikvah* refers to the act of fully sub-
merging yourself in water. There are two kinds of *mikvaot*
(plural of *mikvah*): one constructed to hold a combination of
living water (from rain, a stream, or another natural source)
and tap water; and a natural one (a moving body of water such
as an ocean or river).

Ritual immersion is an obligation for traditionally observant Jewish women and is discussed extensively in the Bible
and the Talmud. Some men participate in *mikvah* before getting married or before holy days, but the ritual is primarily
associated with women. According to traditional Jewish law,
married women enter a *mikvah* seven days after the end of

their menstrual period. They enter in a state of ritual impurity *(tame'ah)*, and leave in a state of ritual purity *(tahara)*. During the period of ritual impurity, traditional women do not touch their husbands in any way; after immersing they reconnect with their partners physically. Since it is linked to a woman's monthly cycle, *mikvah* is strongly tied to fertility and sexuality.

The typical ritual bath is a simply tiled square pool with room for one person. Steps lead down into it, and its water generally rises only about chest high. The attendant—who is present to make sure that you have immersed completely (allowing water to cover every part of your body), and to answer any questions—stands in the room, but outside the *mikvah* pool. While some *mikvaot* are not associated with a particular synagogue but instead are supported by the entire community, others are part of individual synagogues. In some communities, synagogue-based ritual baths serve the needs of all affiliated Jews regardless of the synagogue to which they belong.

The traditional ritual is simple and involves two immersions, going completely beneath the surface with arms and legs spread, fingers loosely held apart, so that the *mikvah* water touches every part of you. Following the first immersion, you come up and say this simple blessing:

Barukh ata Adonai Elohenu Melekh ha-olam asher kidshanu bemitzvotav vetzivanu al-tevillah.
Praised are You, Adonai our God, Sovereign of the universe, who has made us holy with commandments and instructed us concerning immersion.

The second immersion is done without a blessing. It is common practice for women today to immerse a third time and some immerse even more while they pray or petition God to guard those whom they love.

HOW *MIKVAH* IS USED TODAY

The use of *mikvah* is unique among the commandments. While most people think only of the Ten Commandments, there are actually 613 that are included throughout the Torah. Three of the 613 traditional commandments incumbent on Jews are specifically for women: baking and separating challah, lighting Shabbat candles, and the ritual bath. While men can and do bake challah and light Shabbat candles, particularly when there is no woman present, no man can immerse in a ritual bath to sanctify fertility and the cycle of nature that only women experience.

Some liberal Jews regard the traditional practice of visiting the *mikvah* negatively because it frames the time of a woman's menstrual period as one of ritual impurity. At the same time, other liberal Jews are reclaiming this observance and reconceptualizing it as something consonant with their contemporary sensibilities. Some immerse in a *mikvah* to mark the transition into or out of a special or challenging time in their lives, while a smaller number of women observe the obligation to go to a ritual bath in a traditional way. Some women are creating a celebration of wisdom ritual to help them move from midlife to later life, often around the time of their sixtieth birthday. These rituals generally include Bible study, creative readings, some blessings, and testimonials from friends and loved ones. Often there is singing and dancing as well. Some of these women include a visit to the *mikvah* in their celebration, followed by a festive brunch with their closest women friends.

Women are also immersing as a way of healing after physical and emotional trauma—such as a cancer diagnosis and treatment, rape, or a divorce—or to add a spiritual dimension to the medically and emotionally draining process of infertility treatment. They are immersing to mark purely joyful developments, creating extended prewedding *mikvah* rituals and celebrating rabbinic ordination.

Some men, inspired by the mystical aspects of *mikvah,* go to a ritual bath before each Sabbath and prior to the High Holidays in the fall. For them, as for women on a monthly basis, immersion marks the passage and elevation from one spiritual state to another and sanctifies the moment ahead. The ritual bath is also used for men and women as the final step in their conversion to Judaism—a requirement of conversions under Orthodox and Conservative auspices, and used increasingly under Reform.

Mini-*mikvaot* are also being used by some parents in the welcoming ceremony that they hold for their newborn daughters. Water is tied to covenant and faith in the Bible. A famous midrash says that Miriam's faith in God's presence merited the miraculous appearance of a well of water wherever she journeyed with the Israelites in the desert. The association between the *mikvah*'s living waters and the uniquely female cycle of menstruation also makes it a rich symbol to use in a welcoming ceremony for a baby girl, a kind of ritual foreshadowing of her life years down the road.

WRESTLING WITH TRADITION: CONCEPTS OF PURITY AND IMPURITY

For a contemporary Jewish woman, embracing the idea of a ritual bath may be intellectually challenging. Bound up with the idea of immersion are the concepts of ritual impurity and ritual purity, which are rooted in Leviticus. The Bible appears unequivocal: "Do not come near a woman during her period of uncleanness to uncover her nakedness" (Leviticus 18:19). "If a man lies with a woman in her infirmity and uncovers her nakedness, he has laid bare her flow and she has exposed her blood flow; both of them shall be cut off from among their people" (Leviticus 20:18).

It was customary in ancient times for married Jews to abstain from sexual relations during the days a woman was menstruating. Later the Rabbis of the Talmud extended the prohibition for a week after the period ended, and constructed layers of law around it by prohibiting all physical contact between husband and wife for that twelve- to fourteen-day interval.

Mikvah immersion is the apex of the complex set of Jewish laws, called *taharat ha-mishpacha* (literally, "family purity"), observed primarily today only by Orthodox Jews. These laws address sexual interaction between married Jews. They forbid a husband and wife to sleep in the same bed, sit next to each other, or even pass a glass to one another lest they become overcome by desire and transgress the prohibition against sex during the period of ritual impurity. While I appreciate how distance can sharpen desire during the two weeks of separation, I believe that we are able to keep our urges in check without such statutory control. From my perspective, the practice of complete separation also brings with it the sense that a menstruating woman is tainted, that she is dangerously impure.

Susan Handelman, in the book *Total Immersion,* writes: "The laws of *tumah* and *taharah* are suprarational, 'above' reason. And it is precisely because they are of such a high spiritual level, beyond what intellect can comprehend, that they affect an elevated part of the soul, a part of the soul that transcends reason entirely." She also writes: "If we strip the words 'pure' and 'impure' of their physical connotations, and perceive their true spiritual meaning, we see that what they really signify is the presence or absence of holiness." While I don't feel less capable of holiness when menstruating, I do understand menstruation on a spiritual level as the loss of the potential for life, and that it is a time of shedding and preparation for renewal, like the autumn and winter of the body's monthly cycle.

As Rabbi Rachel Sabbath puts it:

> If the waters of the mikvah represent the waters of Eden, where all humanity was first created, then immersing in the mikvah is the closest I can get to that place where we first encountered God. It is a monthly reconnection to the physical experience of the body that God created. It is an opportunity to acknowledge and praise the infinite wisdom and rhythm of the female body.

I embrace the *mikvah* not because I walk into it in any way tainted and emerge somehow purified, but for the other ways that it transforms me and enables me to move fully from one part of my month and my life into the next, in the enduring cycle of which I am but one part.

CHRISTIAN PARALLELS TO *MIKVAH*

Perhaps of all the rituals included in this book, the ritual of *mikvah* has the most obvious Christian parallel: baptism. Just as baptism initiates a person into the church, immersing in a *mikvah* is the final step in becoming a convert to Judaism. As a woman who has finished her menstrual period immerses to become spiritually pure again, so a Christian is baptized in order to become spiritually pure.

Not surprisingly, the practice of baptism originates in the practice of *mikvah*. *Baptizmo* in Greek means simply "to immerse." John the Baptist utilized the practice of immersion for spiritual purity. The Christian Bible records that "John the Baptist appeared in the wilderness preaching a baptism of repentance for the forgiveness of sins" (Mark 1:4). One scholar suggests that John's practice of baptism differs from the Jewish practice of *mikvah* only in that John was only immersing in the river, and not in pools specifically designed for ritual immersion. And John's immersions were for all people, because all people needed purification from sin, while the Torah and the Rabbis require immersion only for people who have come in contact with impure things, such as a woman in contact with menstrual blood.

NOTES

CHAPTER 2: KEEPING KOSHER

1. Moses Maimonides, *The Guide of the Perplexed*, trans. Shlomo Pines (Chicago: University of Chicago Press, 1963), 2:599.
2. Ibid., 2:600.
3. Quoted in Isaac Klein, *A Guide to Jewish Religious Practice* (New York: Jewish Theological Seminary of America, 1979), 303.
4. Samuel Dresner, *The Jewish Dietary Laws*, rev. and exp. ed. (New York: Rabbinical Assembly of America, 1982), 41.
5. Paula Fredriksen, *Jesus of Nazareth, King of the Jews: A Jewish Life and the Emergence of Christianity* (New York: Vintage Books, 1999), 108.
6. Garret Keizer, "A Time to Keep Kosher—Christians Should Adopt Dietary Laws," *Christian Century* April 19–26, 2000, 448.

CHAPTER 4: WRAPPING THE TALLIT (PRAYER SHAWL)

1. Paula Fredriksen, *Jesus of Nazareth, King of the Jews,* 109.

CHAPTER 6: STUDYING TORAH

1. Translation from Lawrence Kushner and Kerry Olitzky, *Sparks beneath the Surface: A Spiritual Commentary on the Torah* (Northvale, N.J.: Jason Aronson, 1993), 107–108.
2. *Megillah* 13b and *Genesis Rabbah* 71:18.

CHAPTER 7: PRAYING DAILY

1. Adapted from Martin Buber, *Tales of the Hasidim: The Early Masters* (New York: Schocken Books, 1975), 69.
2. Quoted in Abraham Joshua Heschel, *Moral Grandeur and Spiritual Audacity: Essays,* ed. Susannah Heschel (New York: Farrar, Straus and Giroux, 1996), 397.
3. Arthur Green and Barry Holtz, eds. and trans., *Your Word Is Fire: The Hasidic Masters on Contemplative Prayer* (Woodstock, Vt.: Jewish Lights Publishing, 1993), 12.
4. Avram Davis, ed. *Meditation from the Heart of Judaism: Today's Teachers Share Their Practices, Techniques, and Faith* (Woodstock, Vt.: Jewish Lights Publishing, 1997), 84.

CHAPTER 8: SAYING GRACE AND NINETY-NINE OTHER BLESSINGS THROUGHOUT THE DAY

1. Abraham Joshua Heschel, *Man's Quest for God: Studies in Prayer and Symbolism* (New York: Macmillan, 1954), 5.
2. *Bereshit Rabbah* 12:6.
3. Lawrence Hoffman, "Jewish and Christian Liturgy," in *Christianity in Jewish Terms,* ed. Tikva Frymer-Kensky (Boulder, Colo.: Westview Press, 2000), 179.

Glossary

Adonai: Literally, "Lord." A euphemism applied to the so-called unpronounceable four-letter name of God (the tetragrammaton).

aliyah: Literally, "going up." Refers to Torah honor; also reference to immigrating to Israel.

Amidah: Literally, "the standing prayer." The central prayer in the liturgy, so named because it is said while standing.

Barekhu: The call to prayer recited in morning *(Shacharit)* and evening *(Maariv)* prayers.

bar mitzvah (plural *b'nei mitzvah*): Rite of passage for thirteen-year-old boys. The term used for a similar ceremony for girls is *bat mitzvah*. In some synagogues, the ceremony for girls takes place at age twelve.

Birkat Hamazon: Grace after meals.

challah: Twisted egg bread used for the Sabbath and holidays.

chuppah: Marriage canopy.

halakhah: Jewish law.

hashkiveinu: Literally, "cause us to lie us down." The name for the prayer recited as part of the bedtime *Shema* ritual. This prayer asks God to "lie us down in peace, and raise us up, O Sovereign, to life."

Hasidism: Anti-intellectualism movement of Jews that originated in Poland in the seventeenth century, led by the charismatic Baal Shem Tov. The movement is best known for its distinctive period garb, including fur-trimmed hats and long black coats. Most well known of the Hasidic communities are the Lubavitcher Hasidim (also known as Chabad).

Havdalah: Brief ritual ceremony that marks the transition between the Sabbath and the rest of the week.

hekhsher: Literally, "validation." Symbol certifying a food product as kosher.

Heschel, Rabbi Abraham Joshua (1907–1972): Philosopher who attempted to illumine the relationship between God and people. This relationship provides the foundation for religion. Heschel articulated a contemporary theology that is the result of the insights he garnered from traditional sources that shed light on contemporary problems and conflicts. He argued that religion has faded in the modern world because we have not attempted to recover the dimension of reality in which a divine encounter might take place.

High Holidays: Rosh Hashanah (New Year) and Yom Kippur (Day of Atonement), so named because of their preeminence in the religious calendar; also called High Holy Days or simply the Holidays.

Kabbalah: Jewish mysticism.

Kaddish Yatom: Literally, "the orphan's Kaddish"; often referred to as the Mourner's Kaddish. Said at the end of every service to commemorate people who have died recently and those people whose *yahrzeit* (anniversary of their death) is being observed.

kashrut: Literally, "fitness" or "propriety." The system of keeping kosher.

kavannah: A meditation said preceding an action, designed to heighten our awareness of and appreciation for the act we are about to perform; also refers to spontaneous (as opposed to fixed) prayers.

kiddush: From the Hebrew word *kadosh,* "to make holy." It is the prayer said over wine, to help usher in the Sabbath day.

kipah: Skull cap; also known by the Yiddish *yarmulke.*

kosher: Fit or proper.

laying tefillin: Yiddish for "putting on" tefillin.

Maariv: The evening service that includes the *Barekhu,* the *Shema,* and the *Shemoneh Esrei.*

Maimonides, Moses (1135–1204): Moses ben Maimon, also called the Rambam, perhaps one of the greatest thinkers in all of Jewish history. Trained as a physician, Maimonides was also a commentator and philosopher. Under the influence of Aristotelian thought as articulated by Arabic philosophers of the middle Ages, he was best known for his *Guide of the Perplexed* and his *Mishneh Torah,* an "easy-to-use" compilation of Jewish law.

mechitzah: The separation in a synagogue that divides the men's section from the women's section.

midrash (plural midrashim): Literally, "to seek." It refers broadly to any interpretation of the Torah, but more often refers to a type of interpretation that is in the form of a story.

mikvah **(plural** *mikvaot***):** Jewish ritual bath.

Mincha: The afternoon service that consists primarily of the *Shemoneh Esrei.*

minyan: Prayer quorum. Traditionally a minyan is required to recite certain prayers publicly, such as the *Barekhu* and the *Shemoneh Esrei.*

Mishnah: Legal codification, expounding the Bible and constituting the core of Oral Law, compiled and edited by Rabbi Judah the Prince in the early part of the third century.

mitzvah (plural *mitzvot***):** Commandment, divine instruction, sacred teaching.

motzi: Hebrew for "the One who brings forth," the main line in the blessing said over bread that initiates a meal.

Old Testament: While Christians refer to the Hebrew Scriptures as the Old Testament, Jews refrain from doing so. Such use would presume that a *new* testament superseded it.

pareve: Yiddish for "neutral." In kashrut, neither milk nor meat.

Shabbat (plural Shabbatot): Hebrew for "Sabbath," sometimes pronounced as *Shabbes* or *Shabbos,* the Ashkenazi Hebrew and Yiddish forms of the same word.

Shacharit: The morning service that is the longest of the three daily services (the other two are *Mincha* and *Maariv*). *Shacharit* contains blessings, recitation of psalms, the *Barekhu,* the *Shema,* and the *Shemoneh Esrei.* On Monday, Thursday, Shabbat, and holidays the Torah is read.

shechitah: [Ritual] slaughter.

Shehecheyanu: Blessing said at *b'nei mitzvah* ceremonies, commencements, retirements, dedications, and other important milestones, as well as in celebrating simple new experiences such as wearing a new suit for the first time.

Shema: The creed in Judaism proclaiming God as one (Deuteronomy 6:4). Added to it are three paragraphs that focus on fulfilling commandments and the Exodus from Egypt (Deuteronomy 6:5–9; Deuteronomy 11:13–21; Numbers 15:37–41).

Shema She-al Hamitah: Literally, "the *Shema* on the bed." The name for the group of prayers said before going to sleep.

Shemoneh Esrei: Literally, "eighteen," referring to the blessing of the *Amidah.* Today it consists of nineteen blessings, which praise, petition, thank, and ask God for forgiveness, health, and prosperity.

Shulchan Arukh: Literally, "the prepared table." A traditional code of Jewish law and practice attributed to Joseph Karo in 1565 C.E., which became authoritative for traditional Judaism.

sukkah: The wooden outdoor booth constructed for the week of the fall holiday of Sukkot. Jews are instructed to dwell in the sukkah during the holiday in remembrance of the booths that the Israelites lived in during the wandering in the wilderness.

tahara: Ritually pure.

tallit gadol: Literally, "large tallit" or "prayer shawl"; originally it meant "gown" or "cloak." Often referred to simply as tallit (plural *tallitot).* Sometimes referred to as *tallis* in the Ashkenazi Hebrew and Yiddish form.

tallit katan: Literally, "small tallit." A four-cornered undergarment; also called *tzitzit* or *arba kanfot* (literally, "four corners").

Talmud: Generally referring to the Babylonian Talmud, the rabbinic discussions called the Gemara along with the Mishnah together is called the Talmud. The Babylonian Talmud was a product of three hundred years of study and was completed around 500 C.E.

tefillah: The Hebrew word for "prayer." It is also the term used in rabbinic literature (the Talmud) that refers to the *Shemoneh Esrei,* or the *Amidah,* the core prayer in the Jewish worship service.

tefillin (singular *tefillah*): Prayer boxes, from the Hebrew word for prayer, in the plural form common to Mishnaic Hebrew.

tikkun: Repair, particularly in the expression *tikkun olam* ("repair of the world").

Torah: First five books of the Bible; the Five Books of Moses; the Pentateuch.

treyf: Literally, "torn." Yiddish for not kosher; in Hebrew *trefah.*

tumah/tame'ah: Ritual impurity/ritually impure.

tzitzit **(plural *tzitziot*):** Fringes on the corners of the tallit, sometimes referred to as *tzitzis* in the Ashkenazi Hebrew form, as well as in Yiddish. Some people consider *tzitzit* as a Jewish form of macramé; sometimes called *arba kanfot*.

yahrzeit: From the Yiddish "year's time" or "time of year," referring to the anniversary of an individual's death, at which time the mourner's kaddish must be recited by family members.

Zohar: A thirteenth-century Jewish mystical classic, known in English as *The Book of Splendor.* The Zohar was written by Moses de Leon in the fourteenth century but was attributed to Shimon Bar Yochai, a figure from the mid-second century.

SUGGESTIONS FOR FURTHER READING

Dresner, Samuel H. *The Jewish Dietary Laws.*, rev. and exp. ed. New York: Rabbinical Assembly of America, 1982.

Greenberg, Irving. *The Jewish Way: Living the Holidays*. New York: Summit Books, 1988.

Hoffman, Lawrence. *The Way into Jewish Prayer*. Woodstock, Vt.: Jewish Lights Publishing, 2000.

———, ed. *My People's Prayer Book: Traditional Prayers, Modern Commentaries*. 10 vols. Woodstock, Vt.: Jewish Lights Publishing, 1997–.

The JPS Torah Commentary. 5 vols. Philadelphia: Jewish Publication Society, 1989–96.

Klein, Isaac. *A Guide to Jewish Religious Practice*. New York: Jewish Theological Seminary of America, 1992.

Kula, Irwin, and Vanessa L. Ochs, eds. *The Book of Jewish Sacred Practices: CLAL's Guide to Everyday and Holiday Rituals and Blessings*. Woodstock, Vt.: Jewish Lights Publishing, 2001.

Kushner, Lawrence, and Nehemia Polen. *Filling Words with Light: Hasidic and Mystical Reflections on Jewish Prayer*. Woodstock, Vt.: Jewish Lights Publishing, 2004.

Mykoff, Moshe, with the Breslov Research Institute. *7th Heaven: Celebrating Shabbat with Rebbe Nachman of Breslov*. Woodstock, Vt.: Jewish Lights Publishing, 2003.

Olitzky, Kerry M., and Ronald Isaacs. *The Complete How To Handbook for Jewish Living.* 3 vols. in 1. Jersey City, N.J.: KTAV Publishing House, 2004.

Plaut, W. Gunther. *The Torah: A Modern Commentary.* New York: UAHC Press, 1981.

Siegel, Richard, Michael Strassfeld, and Sharon Strassfeld. *The Jewish Catalogue: A Do-It-Yourself Kit.* vols. 1 and 2. Philadelphia: Jewish Publication Society, 1973, 1976.

Slonim, Rivkah, ed. *Total Immersion: A Mikvah Anthology.* Northvale, N.J.: Jason Aronson, 1996.

Wolfson, Ron. *Shabbat: The Family Guide to Preparing for and Celebrating the Sabbath.* 2nd ed. Woodstock, Vt.: Jewish Lights Publishing, 2002.

SOME SELECTED PRAYER BOOKS

Conservative: *Siddur Sim Shalom: A Prayerbook for Shabbat, Festivals, and Weekdays.* Rabbi Jules Harlow, ed. and trans. New York: Rabbinical Assembly and United Synagogue of America, 1985. See also *Daily Prayer Book: Ha-Siddur Ha-Shalem.* Philip Birnbaum, trans. New York: Hebrew Publishing Company, 1969.

Orthodox: *The Complete ArtScroll Siddur: Weekday/Sabbath/Festival.* Rabbi Nosson Scherman, trans. Brooklyn: Mesorah Publications, 1984.

Reconstructionist: *Kol HaNeshamah: Shabbat Vehagim.* Wyncote, Pa.: Reconstructionist Press, 1995.

Reform: *Gates of Prayer: The New Union Prayer Book.* New York: Central Conference of American Rabbis, 1975.

CONTRIBUTORS

Debra Nussbaum Cohen is author of *Celebrating Your New Jewish Daughter: Creating Jewish Ways to Welcome Baby Girls into the Covenant* (Jewish Lights) and speaks to synagogue, conference, and Jewish federation groups about how Jewish rituals—new and traditional—can enhance our spiritual lives. She is a religion writer for *New York Jewish Week*, and has written for the *Wall Street Journal*, *New York* magazine, and the *Village Voice*, as well as other Jewish publications.

Rabbi Mark Sameth is the spiritual leader of Pleasantville Community Synagogue in Pleasantville, New York. An essay on his return to Judaism appears in Sid Schwarz's *Finding a Spiritual Home: How a New Generation of Jews Can Transform the American Synagogue* (Jewish Lights). Prior to ordination, he was a rabbinical intern and keyboardist at Congregation B'nai Jeshurun in New York City. A former award-winning country and western songwriter, his songs have been recorded by Loretta Lynn, Ed Bruce, Dickie Lee, and others.

Rabbi Andrew Vogel is spiritual leader of Temple Sinai in Brookline, Massachusetts. Ordained at the Hebrew Union College–Jewish Institute of Religion in New York, he has served as assistant rabbi at Temple Shir Tikva in Wayland, Massachusetts, and at Temple Kol Emeth in Marietta, Georgia. He lives with his wife, Martha Hausman, and their children in the Boston area.

NOTES

Bar/Bat Mitzvah

The Bar/Bat Mitzvah Memory Book
An Album for Treasuring the Spiritual Celebration
By Rabbi Jeffrey K. Salkin and Nina Salkin
A unique album for preserving the spiritual memories of the day, and for recording plans for the Jewish future ahead. Contents include space for creating or
recording family history; teachings received from rabbi, cantor, and others;
mitzvot and *tzedakot* chosen and carried out, etc.
8 x 10, 48 pp, Deluxe Hardcover, 2-color text, ribbon marker, ISBN 1-58023-111-X **$19.95**

Bar/Bat Mitzvah Basics: A Practical Family Guide to Coming of Age Together
Edited by Helen Leneman. Foreword by Rabbi Jeffrey K. Salkin.
6 x 9, 240 pp, Quality PB, ISBN 1-58023-151-9 **$18.95**

For Kids—Putting God on Your Guest List: How to Claim the Spiritual Meaning
of Your Bar or Bat Mitzvah *By Rabbi Jeffrey K. Salkin*
6 x 9, 144 pp, Quality PB, ISBN 1-58023-015-6 **$14.95** *For ages 11–12*

Putting God on the Guest List: How to Reclaim the Spiritual Meaning of Your
Child's Bar or Bat Mitzvah *By Rabbi Jeffrey K. Salkin*
6 x 9, 224 pp, Quality PB, ISBN 1-879045-59-1 **$16.95**

Tough Questions Jews Ask: A Young Adult's Guide to Building a Jewish Life
By Rabbi Edward Feinstein 6 x 9, 160 pp, Quality PB, ISBN 1-58023-139-X **$14.95** *For ages 13 & up*
Also Available: **Tough Questions Jews Ask Teacher's Guide**
8½ x 11, 72 pp, PB, ISBN 1-58023-187-X **$8.95**

Bible Study/Midrash

Hineini in Our Lives: Learning How to Respond to Others through 14 Biblical Texts,
and Personal Stories *By Norman J. Cohen*
6 x 9, 240 pp, Hardcover, ISBN 1-58023-131-4 **$23.95**

Ancient Secrets: Using the Stories of the Bible to Improve Our Everyday Lives
By Rabbi Levi Meier, Ph.D. 5½ x 8½, 288 pp, Quality PB, ISBN 1-58023-064-4 **$16.95**

Moses—The Prince, the Prophet: His Life, Legend & Message for Our Lives
By Rabbi Levi Meier, Ph.D.
6 x 9, 224 pp, Quality PB, ISBN 1-58023-069-5 **$16.95**

Self, Struggle & Change: Family Conflict Stories in Genesis and Their Healing Insights
for Our Lives *By Norman J. Cohen* 6 x 9, 224 pp, Quality PB, ISBN 1-879045-66-4 **$18.99**

Voices from Genesis: Guiding Us through the Stages of Life *By Norman J. Cohen*
6 x 9, 192 pp, Quality PB, ISBN 1-58023-118-7 **$16.95**

Congregation Resources

Becoming a Congregation of Learners: Learning as a Key to Revitalizing
Congregational Life *By Isa Aron, Ph.D. Foreword by Rabbi Lawrence A. Hoffman.*
6 x 9, 304 pp, Quality PB, ISBN 1-58023-089-X **$19.95**

Finding a Spiritual Home: How a New Generation of Jews Can Transform the
American Synagogue *By Rabbi Sidney Schwarz*
6 x 9, 352 pp, Quality PB, ISBN 1-58023-185-3 **$19.95**

Jewish Pastoral Care: A Practical Handbook from Traditional & Contemporary Sources
Edited by Rabbi Dayle A. Friedman 6 x 9, 464 pp, Hardcover, ISBN 1-58023-078-4 **$35.00**

The Self-Renewing Congregation: Organizational Strategies for Revitalizing
Congregational Life *By Isa Aron, Ph.D. Foreword by Dr. Ron Wolfson.*
6 x 9, 304 pp, Quality PB, ISBN 1-58023-166-7 **$19.95**

Children's Books

What You Will See Inside a Synagogue
By Rabbi Lawrence A. Hoffman and Dr. Ron Wolfson; Full-color photos by Bill Aron
A colorful, fun-to-read introduction that explains the ways and whys of Jewish worship and religious life. Full-page photos; concise but informative descriptions of the objects used, the clergy and laypeople who have specific roles, and much more.

8½ x 10½, 32 pp, Full-color photos, Hardcover, ISBN 1-59473-012-1 **$17.99** (A SkyLight Paths book)

Because Nothing Looks Like God
By Lawrence and Karen Kushner
What is God like? Introduces children to the possibilities of spiritual life. Real-life examples of happiness and sadness invite us to explore, together with our children, the questions we all have about God.

11 x 8½, 32 pp, Full-color illus., Hardcover, ISBN 1-58023-092-X **$16.95** For ages 4 & up

Also Available: Because Nothing Looks Like God Teacher's Guide
8½ x 11, 22 pp, PB, ISBN 1-58023-140-3 **$6.95** For ages 5–8

Board Book Companions to Because Nothing Looks Like God
5 x 5, 24 pp, Full-color illus., SkyLight Paths Board Books, **$7.95** each For ages 0–4

What Does God Look Like? ISBN 1-893361-23-3
How Does God Make Things Happen? ISBN 1-893361-24-1
Where Is God? ISBN 1-893361-17-9

The 11th Commandment: Wisdom from Our Children
by The Children of America
"If there were an Eleventh Commandment, what would it be?" Children of many religious denominations across America answer in their own drawings and words.
8 x 10, 48 pp, Full-color illus., Hardcover, ISBN 1-879045-46-X **$16.95** For all ages

Jerusalem of Gold: Jewish Stories of the Enchanted City
Retold by Howard Schwartz. Full-color illus. by Neil Waldman.
A beautiful and engaging collection of historical and legendary stories for children. Based on Talmud, midrash, Jewish folklore, and mystical and Hasidic sources.
8 x 10, 64 pp, Full-color illus., Hardcover, ISBN 1-58023-149-7 **$18.95** For ages 7 & up

The Book of Miracles: A Young Person's Guide to Jewish Spiritual Awareness
By Lawrence Kushner. All-new illustrations by the author.
6 x 9, 96 pp, 2-color illus., Hardcover, ISBN 1-879045-78-8 **$16.95** For ages 9–13

In Our Image: God's First Creatures
By Nancy Sohn Swartz
9 x 12, 32 pp, Full-color illus., Hardcover, ISBN 1-879045-99-0 **$16.95** For ages 4 & up

Also Available as a Board Book: How Did the Animals Help God?
5 x 5, 24 pp, Board, Full-color illus., ISBN 1-59473-044-X **$7.99** For ages 0–4 (A SkyLight Paths book)

From SKYLIGHT PATHS PUBLISHING

Becoming Me: A Story of Creation
By Martin Boroson. Full-color illus. by Christopher Gilvan-Cartwright.
Told in the personal "voice" of the Creator, a story about creation and relationship that is about each one of us.
8 x 10, 32 pp, Full-color illus., Hardcover, ISBN 1-893361-11-X **$16.95** For ages 4 & up

Ten Amazing People: And How They Changed the World
By Maura D. Shaw. Foreword by Dr. Robert Coles. Full-color illus. by Stephen Marchesi.
Black Elk • Dorothy Day • Malcolm X • Mahatma Gandhi • Martin Luther King, Jr. • Mother Teresa • Janusz Korczak • Desmond Tutu • Thich Nhat Hanh • Albert Schweitzer.
8½ x 11, 48 pp, Full-color illus., Hardcover, ISBN 1-893361-47-0 **$17.95** For ages 7 & up

Where Does God Live? By August Gold and Matthew J. Perlman
Helps young readers develop a personal understanding of God.
10 x 8½, 32 pp, Full-color photo illus., Quality PB, ISBN 1-893361-39-X **$8.99** For ages 3–6

Children's Books
by Sandy Eisenberg Sasso

Adam & Eve's First Sunset: God's New Day
Engaging new story explores fear and hope, faith and gratitude in ways that will delight kids and adults—inspiring us to bless each of God's days and nights.
9 x 12, 32 pp, Full-color illus., Hardcover, ISBN 1-58023-177-2 **$17.95** *For ages 4 & up*

But God Remembered
Stories of Women from Creation to the Promised Land
Four different stories of women—Lillith, Serach, Bityah, and the Daughters of Z—teach us important values through their faith and actions.
9 x 12, 32 pp, Full-color illus., Hardcover, ISBN 1-879045-43-5 **$16.95** *For ages 8 & up*

Cain & Abel: Finding the Fruits of Peace
Shows children that we have the power to deal with anger in positive ways. Provides questions for kids and adults to explore together.
9 x 12, 32 pp, Full-color illus., Hardcover, ISBN 1-58023-123-3 **$16.95** *For ages 5 & up*

God in Between
If you wanted to find God, where would you look? This magical, mythical tale teaches that God can be found where we are: within all of us and the relationships between us.
9 x 12, 32 pp, Full-color illus., Hardcover, ISBN 1-879045-86-9 **$16.95** *For ages 4 & up*

God's Paintbrush: Special 10th Anniversary Edition
Wonderfully interactive, invites children of all faiths and backgrounds to encounter God through moments in their own lives. Provides questions adult and child can explore together.
11 x 8½, 32 pp, Full-color illus., Hardcover, ISBN 1-58023-195-0 **$17.95** *For ages 4 & up*

Also Available: **God's Paintbrush Teacher's Guide**
8½ x 11, 32 pp, PB, ISBN 1-879045-57-5 **$8.95**

God's Paintbrush Celebration Kit
A Spiritual Activity Kit for Teachers and Students of All Faiths, All Backgrounds
Additional activity sheets available:
8-Student Activity Sheet Pack (40 sheets/5 sessions), ISBN 1-58023-058-X **$19.95**
Single-Student Activity Sheet Pack (5 sessions), ISBN 1-58023-059-8 **$3.95**

In God's Name
Like an ancient myth in its poetic text and vibrant illustrations, this award-winning modern fable about the search for God's name celebrates the diversity and, at the same time, the unity of all people.
9 x 12, 32 pp, Full-color illus., Hardcover, ISBN 1-879045-26-5 **$16.99** *For ages 4 & up*

Also Available as a Board Book: **What Is God's Name?**
5 x 5, 24 pp, Board, Full-color illus., ISBN 1-893361-10-1 **$7.99** *For ages 0–4 (A SkyLight Paths book)*

Also Available: **In God's Name video and study guide**
Computer animation, original music, and children's voices. 18 min. **$29.99**

Also Available in Spanish: **El nombre de Dios**
9 x 12, 32 pp, Full-color illus., Hardcover, ISBN 1-893361-63-2 **$16.95** *(A SkyLight Paths book)*

Noah's Wife: The Story of Naamah
When God tells Noah to bring the animals of the world onto the ark, God also calls on Naamah, Noah's wife, to save each plant on Earth. Based on an ancient text.
9 x 12, 32 pp, Full-color illus., Hardcover, ISBN 1-58023-134-9 **$16.95** *For ages 4 & up*

Also Available as a Board Book: **Naamah, Noah's Wife**
5 x 5, 24 pp, Full-color illus., Board, ISBN 1-893361-56-X **$7.95** *For ages 0–4 (A SkyLight Paths book)*

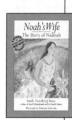

For Heaven's Sake: Finding God in Unexpected Places
9 x 12, 32 pp, Full-color illus., Hardcover, ISBN 1-58023-054-7 **$16.95** *For ages 4 & up*

God Said Amen: Finding the Answers to Our Prayers
9 x 12, 32 pp, Full-color illus., Hardcover, ISBN 1-58023-080-6 **$16.95** *For ages 4 & up*

Current Events/History

The Story of the Jews: A 4,000-Year Adventure—A Graphic History Book
Written & illustrated by Stan Mack
Through witty, illustrated narrative, we visit all the major happenings from biblical times to the twenty-first century. Celebrates the major characters and events that have shaped the Jewish people and culture.
6 x 9, 288 pp., illus., Quality PB, ISBN 1-58023-155-1 **$16.95**

The Jewish Prophet: Visionary Words from Moses and Miriam to Henrietta Szold and A. J. Heschel *By Rabbi Michael J. Shire*
6½ x 8½, 128 pp, 123 full-color illus., Hardcover, ISBN 1-58023-168-3 **$25.00**

Shared Dreams: Martin Luther King, Jr. & the Jewish Community
By Rabbi Marc Schneier. Preface by Martin Luther King III.
6 x 9, 240 pp, Hardcover, ISBN 1-58023-062-8 **$24.95**

"Who Is a Jew?": Conversations, Not Conclusions *By Meryl Hyman*
6 x 9, 272 pp, Quality PB, ISBN 1-58023-052-0 **$16.95**

Ecology

Ecology & the Jewish Spirit: Where Nature & the Sacred Meet
Edited by Ellen Bernstein 6 x 9, 288 pp, Quality PB, ISBN 1-58023-082-2 **$16.95**

Torah of the Earth: Exploring 4,000 Years of Ecology in Jewish Thought
Vol. 1: Biblical Israel: One Land, One People; Rabbinic Judaism: One People, Many Lands
Vol. 2: Zionism: One Land, Two Peoples; Eco-Judaism: One Earth, Many Peoples
Edited by Rabbi Arthur Waskow
Vol. 1: 6 x 9, 272 pp, Quality PB, ISBN 1-58023-086-5 **$19.95**
Vol. 2: 6 x 9, 336 pp, Quality PB, ISBN 1-58023-087-3 **$19.95**

Grief/Healing

Against the Dying of the Light: A Parent's Story of Love, Loss and Hope
By Leonard Fein
In this unusual exploration of heartbreak and healing, Leonard Fein chronicles the sudden death of his 30-year-old daughter and shares the hard-earned wisdom that emerges in the face of loss and grief.
5½ x 8½, 176 pp, Quality PB, ISBN 1-58023-197-7 **$15.99**

Grief in Our Seasons: A Mourner's Kaddish Companion *By Rabbi Kerry M. Olitzky*
4½ x 6½, 448 pp, Quality PB, ISBN 1-879045-55-9 **$15.95**

Healing of Soul, Healing of Body: Spiritual Leaders Unfold the Strength & Solace in Psalms *Edited by Rabbi Simkha Y. Weintraub, C.S.W.*
6 x 9, 128 pp, 2-color illus. text, Quality PB, ISBN 1-879045-31-1 **$14.95**

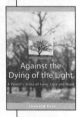

Jewish Paths toward Healing and Wholeness: A Personal Guide to Dealing with Suffering *By Rabbi Kerry M. Olitzky. Foreword by Debbie Friedman.*
6 x 9, 192 pp, Quality PB, ISBN 1-58023-068-7 **$15.95**

Mourning & Mitzvah, 2nd Edition: A Guided Journal for Walking the Mourner's Path through Grief to Healing *By Anne Brener, L.C.S.W.*
7½ x 9, 304 pp, Quality PB, ISBN 1-58023-113-6 **$19.95**

The Perfect Stranger's Guide to Funerals and Grieving Practices
A Guide to Etiquette in Other People's Religious Ceremonies *Edited by Stuart M. Matlins*
6 x 9, 240 pp, Quality PB, ISBN 1-893361-20-9 **$16.95** (A SkyLight Paths book)

Tears of Sorrow, Seeds of Hope: A Jewish Spiritual Companion for Infertility and Pregnancy Loss *By Rabbi Nina Beth Cardin*
6 x 9, 192 pp, Hardcover, ISBN 1-58023-017-2 **$19.95**

A Time to Mourn, A Time to Comfort: A Guide to Jewish Bereavement and Comfort *By Dr. Ron Wolfson* 7 x 9, 336 pp, Quality PB, ISBN 1-879045-96-6 **$18.95**

When a Grandparent Dies: A Kid's Own Remembering Workbook for Dealing with Shiva and the Year Beyond *By Nechama Liss-Levinson, Ph.D.*
8 x 10, 48 pp, 2-color text, Hardcover, ISBN 1-879045-44-3 **$15.95** *For ages 7–13*

Abraham Joshua Heschel

The Earth Is the Lord's: The Inner World of the Jew in Eastern Europe
5½ x 8, 128 pp, Quality PB, ISBN 1-879045-42-7 **$14.95**

Israel: An Echo of Eternity *New Introduction by Susannah Heschel*
5½ x 8, 272 pp, Quality PB, ISBN 1-879045-70-2 **$19.95**

A Passion for Truth: Despair and Hope in Hasidism
5½ x 8, 352 pp, Quality PB, ISBN 1-879045-41-9 **$18.99**

Holidays/Holy Days

Reclaiming Judaism as a Spiritual Practice
Holy Days and Shabbat
By Rabbi Goldie Milgram
Provides a framework for understanding the powerful and often unexplained intellectual, emotional, and spiritual tools that are essential for a lively, relevant, and fulfilling Jewish spiritual practice. 7 x 9, 272 pp, Quality PB, ISBN 1-58023-205-1 **$19.99**

7th Heaven: Celebrating Shabbat with Rebbe Nachman of Breslov
By Moshe Mykoff with the Breslov Research Institute
Based on the teachings of Rebbe Nachman of Breslov. Explores the art of consciously observing Shabbat and understanding in-depth many of the day's traditional spiritual practices. 5⅛ x 8¼, 224 pp, Deluxe PB w/flaps, ISBN 1-58023-175-6 **$18.95**

The Women's Passover Companion
Women's Reflections on the Festival of Freedom
Edited by Rabbi Sharon Cohen Anisfeld, Tara Mohr, and Catherine Spector
Groundbreaking. A provocative conversation about women's relationships to Passover as well as the roots and meanings of women's seders.
6 x 9, 352 pp, Hardcover, ISBN 1-58023-128-4 **$24.95**

The Women's Seder Sourcebook
Rituals & Readings for Use at the Passover Seder
Edited by Rabbi Sharon Cohen Anisfeld, Tara Mohr, and Catherine Spector
Gathers the voices of more than one hundred women in readings, personal and creative reflections, commentaries, blessings, and ritual suggestions that can be incorporated into your Passover celebration as supplements to or substitutes for traditional passages of the haggadah.
6 x 9, 384 pp, Hardcover, ISBN 1-58023-136-5 **$24.95**

Creating Lively Passover Seders: A Sourcebook of Engaging Tales, Texts & Activities *By David Arnow, Ph.D.* 7 x 9, 416 pp, Quality PB, ISBN 1-58023-184-5 **$24.99**

Hanukkah, 2nd Edition: The Family Guide to Spiritual Celebration
By Dr. Ron Wolfson. Edited by Joel Lurie Grishaver.
7 x 9, 240 pp, illus., Quality PB, ISBN 1-58023-122-5 **$18.95**

The Jewish Family Fun Book: Holiday Projects, Everyday Activities, and Travel Ideas with Jewish Themes *By Danielle Dardashti and Roni Sarig. Illus. by Avi Katz.*
6 x 9, 288 pp, 70+ b/w illus. & diagrams, Quality PB, ISBN 1-58023-171-3 **$18.95**

The Jewish Gardening Cookbook: Growing Plants & Cooking for Holidays & Festivals *By Michael Brown*
6 x 9, 224 pp, 30+ illus., Quality PB, ISBN 1-58023-116-0 **$16.95**

The Jewish Lights Book of Fun Classroom Activities: Simple and Seasonal Projects for Teachers and Students *By Danielle Dardashti and Roni Sarig*
6 x 9, 240 pp, Quality PB, ISBN 1-58023-206-X **$19.99**

Passover, 2nd Edition: The Family Guide to Spiritual Celebration
By Dr. Ron Wolfson with Joel Lurie Grishaver 7 x 9, 352 pp, Quality PB, ISBN 1-58023-174-8 **$19.95**

Shabbat, 2nd Edition: The Family Guide to Preparing for and Celebrating the Sabbath
By Dr. Ron Wolfson 7 x 9, 320 pp, illus., Quality PB, ISBN 1-58023-164-0 **$19.95**

Sharing Blessings: Children's Stories for Exploring the Spirit of the Jewish Holidays
By Rahel Musleah and Michael Klayman
8½ x 11, 64 pp, Full-color illus., Hardcover, ISBN 1-879045-71-0 **$18.95** *For ages 6 & up*

Inspiration

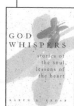

God in All Moments
Mystical & Practical Spiritual Wisdom from Hasidic Masters
Edited and translated by Or N. Rose with Ebn D. Leader
Hasidic teachings on how to be mindful in religious practice and cultivating every-day ethical behavior—*hanhagot*. 5½ x 8½, 192 pp, Quality PB, ISBN 1-58023-186-1 **$16.95**

Our Dance with God: Finding Prayer, Perspective and Meaning in the Stories of Our Lives *By Karyn D. Kedar*
Inspiring spiritual insight to guide you on your life journeys and teach you to live and thrive in two conflicting worlds: the rational/material and the spiritual.
6 x 9, 176 pp, Quality PB, ISBN 1-58023-202-7 **$16.99**

Also Available: **The Dance of the Dolphin** (Hardcover edition of *Our Dance with God*)
6 x 9, 176 pp, Hardcover, ISBN 1-58023-154-3 **$19.95**

The Empty Chair: Finding Hope and Joy—Timeless Wisdom from a Hasidic Master, Rebbe Nachman of Breslov *Adapted by Moshe Mykoff and the Breslov Research Institute*
4 x 6, 128 pp, 2-color text, Deluxe PB w/flaps, ISBN 1-879045-67-2 **$9.95**

The Gentle Weapon: Prayers for Everyday and Not-So-Everyday Moments—Timeless Wisdom from the Teachings of the Hasidic Master, Rebbe Nachman of Breslov
Adapted by Moshe Mykoff and S. C. Mizrahi, together with the Breslov Research Institute
4 x 6, 144 pp, 2-color text, Deluxe PB w/flaps, ISBN 1-58023-022-9 **$9.95**

God Whispers: Stories of the Soul, Lessons of the Heart *By Karyn D. Kedar*
6 x 9, 176 pp, Quality PB, ISBN 1-58023-088-1 **$15.95**

An Orphan in History: One Man's Triumphant Search for His Jewish Roots
By Paul Cowan. Afterword by Rachel Cowan. 6 x 9, 288 pp, Quality PB, ISBN 1-58023-135-7 **$16.95**

Restful Reflections: Nighttime Inspiration to Calm the Soul, Based on Jewish Wisdom
By Rabbi Kerry M. Olitzky & Rabbi Lori Forman 4½ x 6¼, 448 pp, Quality PB, ISBN 1-58023-091-1 **$15.95**

Sacred Intentions: Daily Inspiration to Strengthen the Spirit, Based on Jewish Wisdom
By Rabbi Kerry M. Olitzky and Rabbi Lori Forman 4½ x 6¼, 448 pp, Quality PB, ISBN 1-58023-061-X **$15.95**

Kabbalah/Mysticism/Enneagram

Seek My Face: A Jewish Mystical Theology
By Dr. Arthur Green
This classic work of contemporary Jewish theology, revised and updated, is a profound, deeply personal statement of the lasting truths of Jewish mysticism and the basic faith claims of Judaism. A tool for anyone seeking the elusive presence of God in the world. 6 x 9, 304 pp, Quality PB, ISBN 1-58023-130-6 **$19.95**

Zohar: Annotated & Explained
Translation and annotation by Dr. Daniel C. Matt. Foreword by Andrew Harvey
Offers insightful yet unobtrusive commentary to the masterpiece of Jewish mysticism that explains references and mystical symbols, shares wisdom of spiritual masters, and clarifies the *Zohar*'s bold claim: We have always been taught that we need God, but in order to manifest in the world, God needs us.
5½ x 8½, 160 pp, Quality PB, ISBN 1-893361-51-9 **$15.99** (A SkyLight Paths book)

Cast in God's Image: Discover Your Personality Type Using the Enneagram and Kabbalah
By Rabbi Howard A. Addison
7 x 9, 176 pp, Quality PB, Layflat binding, 20+ journaling exercises, ISBN 1-58023-124-1 **$16.95**

Ehyeh: A Kabbalah for Tomorrow *By Dr. Arthur Green*
6 x 9, 224 pp, Quality PB, ISBN 1-58023-213-2 **$16.99**; Hardcover, ISBN 1-58023-125-X **$21.99**

The Enneagram and Kabbalah: Reading Your Soul *By Rabbi Howard A. Addison*
6 x 9, 176 pp, Quality PB, ISBN 1-58023-001-6 **$15.95**

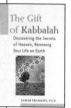

Finding Joy: A Practical Spiritual Guide to Happiness *By Dannel I. Schwartz with Mark Hass*
6 x 9, 192 pp, Quality PB, ISBN 1-58023-009-1 **$14.95**; Hardcover, ISBN 1-879045-53-2 **$19.95**

The Gift of Kabbalah: Discovering the Secrets of Heaven, Renewing Your Life on Earth
By Tamar Frankiel, Ph.D.
6 x 9, 256 pp, Quality PB, ISBN 1-58023-141-1 **$16.95**; Hardcover, ISBN 1-58023-108-X **$21.95**

The Way Into Jewish Mystical Tradition *By Lawrence Kushner*
6 x 9, 224 pp, Quality PB, ISBN 1-58023-200-0 **$18.99**; Hardcover, ISBN 1-58023-029-6 **$21.95**

Life Cycle
Marriage / Parenting / Family / Aging

Jewish Fathers: A Legacy of Love
Photographs by Lloyd Wolf. Essays by Paula Wolfson. Foreword by Harold S. Kushner.
Honors the role of contemporary Jewish fathers in America. Each father tells in his own words what it means to be a parent and Jewish, and what he learned from his own father. Insightful photos. 9½ x 9⅞, 144 pp with 100+ duotone photos, Hardcover, ISBN 1-58023-204-3 **$30.00**

The New Jewish Baby Album: Creating and Celebrating the Beginning of a Spiritual Life—A Jewish Lights Companion
By the Editors at Jewish Lights. Foreword by Anita Diamant. Preface by Sandy Eisenberg Sasso.
A spiritual keepsake that will be treasured for generations. More than just a memory book, *shows you how—and why it's important*—to create a Jewish home and a Jewish life. 8 x 10, 64 pp, Deluxe Padded Hardcover, Full-color illus., ISBN 1-58023-138-1 **$19.95**

The Jewish Pregnancy Book: A Resource for the Soul, Body & Mind during Pregnancy, Birth & the First Three Months
By Sandy Falk, M.D., and Rabbi Daniel Judson, with Steven A. Rapp
Includes medical information on fetal development, pre-natal testing and more, from a liberal Jewish perspective; prenatal *Aleph-Bet* yoga; and prayers and rituals for each stage of pregnancy. 7 x 10, 208 pp, Quality PB, b/w illus., ISBN 1-58023-178-0 **$16.95**

Celebrating Your New Jewish Daughter: Creating Jewish Ways to Welcome Baby Girls into the Covenant—New and Traditional Ceremonies
By Debra Nussbaum Cohen 6 x 9, 272 pp, Quality PB, ISBN 1-58023-090-3 **$18.95**

The New Jewish Baby Book: Names, Ceremonies & Customs—A Guide for Today's Families *By Anita Diamant* 6 x 9, 336 pp, Quality PB, ISBN 1-879045-28-1 **$18.95**

Parenting As a Spiritual Journey: Deepening Ordinary and Extraordinary Events into Sacred Occasions *By Rabbi Nancy Fuchs-Kreimer* 6 x 9, 224 pp, Quality PB, ISBN 1-58023-016-4 **$16.95**

Embracing the Covenant: Converts to Judaism Talk About Why & How
Edited and with introductions by Rabbi Allan Berkowitz and Patti Moskovitz
6 x 9, 192 pp, Quality PB, ISBN 1-879045-50-8 **$16.95**

The Guide to Jewish Interfaith Family Life: An InterfaithFamily.com Handbook
Edited by Ronnie Friedland and Edmund Case 6 x 9, 384 pp, Quality PB, ISBN 1-58023-153-5 **$18.95**

Introducing My Faith and My Community
The Jewish Outreach Institute Guide for the Christian in a Jewish Interfaith Relationship
By Rabbi Kerry M. Olitzky 6 x 9, 176 pp, Quality PB, ISBN 1-58023-192-6 **$16.99**

Making a Successful Jewish Interfaith Marriage: The Jewish Outreach Institute Guide to Opportunities, Challenges and Resources
By Rabbi Kerry M. Olitzky with Joan Peterson Littman 6 x 9, 176 pp, Quality PB, ISBN 1-58023-170-5 **$16.95**

How to Be a Perfect Stranger, 3rd Edition: The Essential Religious Etiquette Handbook *Edited by Stuart M. Matlins and Arthur J. Magida*
The indispensable guide to the rituals and celebrations of the major religions and denominations in North America from the perspective of an interested guest of any other faith. 6 x 9, 432 pp, Quality PB, ISBN 1-893361-67-5 **$19.95** *(A SkyLight Paths book)*

The Creative Jewish Wedding Book: A Hands-On Guide to New & Old Traditions, Ceremonies & Celebrations *By Gabrielle Kaplan-Mayer*
Provides the tools to create the most meaningful Jewish traditional or alternative wedding by using ritual elements to express your unique style and spirituality. 9 x 9, 288 pp, b/w photos, Quality PB, ISBN 1-58023-194-2 **$19.99**

Divorce Is a Mitzvah: A Practical Guide to Finding Wholeness and Holiness When Your Marriage Dies *By Rabbi Perry Netter. Afterword by Rabbi Laura Geller.*
6 x 9, 224 pp, Quality PB, ISBN 1-58023-172-1 **$16.95**

A Heart of Wisdom: Making the Jewish Journey from Midlife through the Elder Years
Edited by Susan Berrin. Foreword by Harold Kushner. 6 x 9, 384 pp, Quality PB, ISBN 1-58023-051-2 **$18.95**

So That Your Values Live On: Ethical Wills and How to Prepare Them
Edited by Jack Riemer and Nathaniel Stampfer 6 x 9, 272 pp, Quality PB, ISBN 1-879045-34-6 **$18.95**

Meditation

The Handbook of Jewish Meditation Practices
A Guide for Enriching the Sabbath and Other Days of Your Life
By Rabbi David A. Cooper
Easy-to-learn meditation techniques for use on the Sabbath and every day, to help us return to the roots of traditional Jewish spirituality where Shabbat is a state of mind and soul. 6 x 9, 208 pp, Quality PB, ISBN 1-58023-102-0 **$16.95**

Discovering Jewish Meditation: Instruction & Guidance for Learning an Ancient
Spiritual Practice *By Nan Fink Gefen, Ph.D.* 6 x 9, 208 pp, Quality PB, ISBN 1-58023-067-9 **$16.95**

A Heart of Stillness: A Complete Guide to Learning the Art of Meditation
By Rabbi David A. Cooper 5½ x 8½, 272 pp, Quality PB, ISBN 1-893361-03-9 **$16.95**
(A SkyLight Paths book)

Meditation from the Heart of Judaism: Today's Teachers Share Their
Practices, Techniques, and Faith *Edited by Avram Davis*
6 x 9, 256 pp, Quality PB, ISBN 1-58023-049-0 **$16.95**

Silence, Simplicity & Solitude: A Complete Guide to Spiritual Retreat at Home
By Rabbi David A. Cooper 5½ x 8½, 336 pp, Quality PB, ISBN 1-893361-04-7 **$16.95**
(A SkyLight Paths book)

Three Gates to Meditation Practice: A Personal Journey into Sufism,
Buddhism, and Judaism *By Rabbi David A. Cooper*
5½ x 8½, 240 pp, Quality PB, ISBN 1-893361-22-5 **$16.95** *(A SkyLight Paths book)*

The Way of Flame: A Guide to the Forgotten Mystical Tradition of Jewish Meditation
By Avram Davis 4½ x 8, 176 pp, Quality PB, ISBN 1-58023-060-1 **$15.95**

Ritual/Sacred Practice/Journaling

The Jewish Dream Book: The Key to Opening the Inner Meaning of
Your Dreams *By Vanessa L. Ochs with Elizabeth Ochs; Full-color illus. by Kristina Swarner*
Instructions for how modern people can perform ancient Jewish dream practices and dream interpretations drawn from the Jewish wisdom tradition. For anyone who wants to understand their dreams—and themselves.
8 x 8, 120 pp, Full-color illus., Deluxe PB w/flaps, ISBN 1-58023-132-2 **$16.95**

The Jewish Journaling Book: How to Use Jewish Tradition to Write
Your Life & Explore Your Soul *By Janet Ruth Falon*
Details the history of Jewish journaling throughout biblical and modern times, and teaches specific journaling techniques to help you create and maintain a vital journal, from a Jewish perspective. 8 x 8, 304 pp, Deluxe PB w/flaps, ISBN 1-58023-203-5 **$18.99**

The Rituals & Practices of a Jewish Life: A Handbook for Personal Spiritual
Renewal *Edited by Rabbi Kerry M. Olitzky and Rabbi Daniel Judson*
6 x 9, 272 pp, illus., Quality PB, ISBN 1-58023-169-1 **$18.95**

The Book of Jewish Sacred Practices: CLAL's Guide to Everyday & Holiday
Rituals & Blessings *Edited by Rabbi Irwin Kula and Vanessa L. Ochs, Ph.D.*
6 x 9, 368 pp, Quality PB, ISBN 1-58023-152-7 **$18.95**

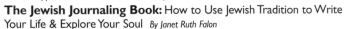

Science Fiction/
Mystery & Detective Fiction

Mystery Midrash: An Anthology of Jewish Mystery & Detective Fiction
Edited by Lawrence W. Raphael. Preface by Joel Siegel.
6 x 9, 304 pp, Quality PB, ISBN 1-58023-055-5 **$16.95**

Criminal Kabbalah: An Intriguing Anthology of Jewish Mystery & Detective Fiction
Edited by Lawrence W. Raphael. Foreword by Laurie R. King.
6 x 9, 256 pp, Quality PB, ISBN 1-58023-109-8 **$16.95**

More Wandering Stars: An Anthology of Outstanding Stories of Jewish Fantasy and
Science Fiction *Edited by Jack Dann. Introduction by Isaac Asimov.*
6 x 9, 192 pp, Quality PB, ISBN 1-58023-063-6 **$16.95**

Wandering Stars: An Anthology of Jewish Fantasy & Science Fiction
Edited by Jack Dann. Introduction by Isaac Asimov.
6 x 9, 272 pp, Quality PB, ISBN 1-58023-005-9 **$16.95**

Spirituality

The Alphabet of Paradise: An A–Z of Spirituality for Everyday Life
By Rabbi Howard Cooper
In twenty-six engaging chapters, Cooper spiritually illuminates the subjects of our daily lives—A to Z—examining these sources by using an ancient Jewish mystical method of interpretation that reveals both the literal and more allusive meanings of each. 5 x 7¾, 224 pp, Quality PB, ISBN 1-893361-80-2 **$16.95** *(A SkyLight Paths book)*

Does the Soul Survive?: A Jewish Journey to Belief in Afterlife, Past Lives & Living with Purpose   *By Rabbi Elie Kaplan Spitz. Foreword by Brian L Weiss, M.D.*
Spitz relates his own experiences and those shared with him by people he has worked with as a rabbi, and shows us that belief in afterlife and past lives, so often approached with reluctance, is in fact true to Jewish tradition.
6 x 9, 288 pp, Quality PB, ISBN 1-58023-165-9 **$16.99**; Hardcover, ISBN 1-58023-094-6 **$21.95**

First Steps to a New Jewish Spirit: Reb Zalman's Guide to Recapturing the Intimacy & Ecstasy in Your Relationship with God
By Rabbi Zalman M. Schachter-Shalomi with Donald Gropman
An extraordinary spiritual handbook that restores psychic and physical vigor by introducing us to new models and alternative ways of practicing Judaism. Offers meditation and contemplation exercises for enriching the most important aspects of everyday life.   6 x 9, 144 pp, Quality PB, ISBN 1-58023-182-9 **$16.95**

God in Our Relationships: Spirituality between People from the Teachings of Martin Buber   *By Rabbi Dennis S. Ross*
On the eightieth anniversary of Buber's classic work, we can discover new answers to critical issues in our lives. Inspiring examples from Ross's own life—as congregational rabbi, father, hospital chaplain, social worker, and husband—illustrate Buber's difficult-to-understand ideas about how we encounter God and each other. 5½ x 8½, 160 pp, Quality PB, ISBN 1-58023-147-0 **$16.95**

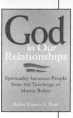

The Jewish Lights Spirituality Handbook: A Guide to Understanding, Exploring & Living a Spiritual Life   *Edited by Stuart M. Matlins*
What exactly is "Jewish" about spirituality? How do I make it a part of my life? Fifty of today's foremost spiritual leaders share their ideas and experience with us.
6 x 9, 456 pp, Quality PB, ISBN 1-58023-093-8 **$19.99**; Hardcover, ISBN 1-58023-100-4 **$24.95**

Bringing the Psalms to Life: How to Understand and Use the Book of Psalms
By Dr. Daniel F. Polish
6 x 9, 208 pp, Quality PB, ISBN 1-58023-157-8 **$16.95**; Hardcover, ISBN 1-58023-077-6 **$21.95**

God & the Big Bang: Discovering Harmony between Science & Spirituality
By Dr. Daniel C. Matt 6 x 9, 216 pp, Quality PB, ISBN 1-879045-89-3 **$16.95**

Godwrestling—Round 2: Ancient Wisdom, Future Paths
By Rabbi Arthur Waskow 6 x 9, 352 pp, Quality PB, ISBN 1-879045-72-9 **$18.95**

One God Clapping: The Spiritual Path of a Zen Rabbi   *By Rabbi Alan Lew with Sherril Jaffe*
5½ x 8½, 336 pp, Quality PB, ISBN 1-58023-115-2 **$16.95**

The Path of Blessing: Experiencing the Energy and Abundance of the Divine
By Rabbi Marcia Prager 5½ x 8½, 240 pp, Quality PB, ISBN 1-58023-148-9 **$16.95**

Six Jewish Spiritual Paths: A Rationalist Looks at Spirituality   *By Rabbi Rifat Sonsino*
6 x 9, 208 pp, Quality PB, ISBN 1-58023-167-5 **$16.95**; Hardcover, ISBN 1-58023-095-4 **$21.95**

Soul Judaism: Dancing with God into a New Era
By Rabbi Wayne Dosick 5½ x 8½, 304 pp, Quality PB, ISBN 1-58023-053-9 **$16.95**

Stepping Stones to Jewish Spiritual Living: Walking the Path Morning, Noon, and Night   *By Rabbi James L. Mirel and Karen Bonnell Werth*
6 x 9, 240 pp, Quality PB, ISBN 1-58023-074-1 **$16.95**; Hardcover, ISBN 1-58023-003-2 **$21.95**

There Is No Messiah... and You're It: The Stunning Transformation of Judaism's Most Provocative Idea   *By Rabbi Robert N. Levine, D.D.*
6 x 9, 192 pp, Hardcover, ISBN 1-58023-173-X **$21.95**

These Are the Words: A Vocabulary of Jewish Spiritual Life   *By Dr. Arthur Green*
6 x 9, 304 pp, Quality PB, ISBN 1-58023-107-1 **$18.95**

Spirituality/Lawrence Kushner

The Book of Letters: A Mystical Hebrew Alphabet
Popular Hardcover Edition, 6 x 9, 80 pp, 2-color text, ISBN 1-879045-00-1 **$24.95**
Deluxe Gift Edition with slipcase, 9 x 12, 80 pp, 4-color text, Hardcover, ISBN 1-879045-01-X **$79.95**
Collector's Limited Edition, 9 x 12, 80 pp, gold foil embossed pages, w/limited edition silkscreened print, ISBN 1-879045-04-4 **$349.00**

The Book of Miracles: A Young Person's Guide to Jewish Spiritual Awareness
All-new illustrations by the author
6 x 9, 96 pp, 2-color illus., Hardcover, ISBN 1-879045-78-8 **$16.95** *For ages 9–13*

The Book of Words: Talking Spiritual Life, Living Spiritual Talk
6 x 9, 160 pp, Quality PB, ISBN 1-58023-020-2 **$16.95**

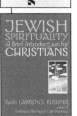

Eyes Remade for Wonder: A Lawrence Kushner Reader
Introduction by Thomas Moore
6 x 9, 240 pp, Quality PB, ISBN 1-58023-042-3 **$18.95;** Hardcover, ISBN 1-58023-014-8 **$23.95**

God Was in This Place & I, i Did Not Know
Finding Self, Spirituality and Ultimate Meaning
6 x 9, 192 pp, Quality PB, ISBN 1-879045-33-8 **$16.95**

Honey from the Rock: An Introduction to Jewish Mysticism
6 x 9, 176 pp, Quality PB, ISBN 1-58023-073-3 **$16.95**

Invisible Lines of Connection: Sacred Stories of the Ordinary
5½ x 8½, 160 pp, Quality PB, ISBN 1-879045-98-2 **$15.95**

Jewish Spirituality—A Brief Introduction for Christians
5½ x 8½, 112 pp, Quality PB Original, ISBN 1-58023-150-0 **$12.95**

The River of Light: Jewish Mystical Awareness
6 x 9, 192 pp, Quality PB, ISBN 1-58023-096-2 **$16.95**

The Way Into Jewish Mystical Tradition
6 x 9, 224 pp, Quality PB, ISBN 1-58023-200-0 **$18.99;** Hardcover, ISBN 1-58023-029-6 **$21.95**

Spirituality/Prayer

Pray Tell: A Hadassah Guide to Jewish Prayer
By Rabbi Jules Harlow, with contributions from Tamara Cohen, Rochelle Furstenberg, Rabbi Daniel Gordis, Leora Tanenbaum, and many others

A guide to traditional Jewish prayer enriched with insight and wisdom from a broad variety of viewpoints—from Orthodox, Conservative, Reform, and Reconstructionist Judaism to New Age and feminist.
8½ x 11, 400 pp, Quality PB, ISBN 1-58023-163-2 **$29.95**

My People's Prayer Book Series
Traditional Prayers, Modern Commentaries
Edited by Rabbi Lawrence A. Hoffman

Provides diverse and exciting commentary to the traditional liturgy, helping modern men and women find new wisdom in Jewish prayer, and bring liturgy into their lives.

Each book includes Hebrew text, modern translation, and commentaries from all perspectives of the Jewish world.
Vol. 1—The *Sh'ma* and Its Blessings
7 x 10, 168 pp, Hardcover, ISBN 1-879045-79-6 **$23.95**
Vol. 2—The *Amidah*
7 x 10, 240 pp, Hardcover, ISBN 1-879045-80-X **$24.95**
Vol. 3—*P'sukei D'zimrah* (Morning Psalms)
7 x 10, 240 pp, Hardcover, ISBN 1-879045-81-8 **$24.95**
Vol. 4—*Seder K'riat Hatorah* (The Torah Service)
7 x 10, 264 pp, Hardcover, ISBN 1-879045-82-6 **$23.95**
Vol. 5—*Birkhot Hashachar* (Morning Blessings)
7 x 10, 240 pp, Hardcover, ISBN 1-879045-83-4 **$24.95**
Vol. 6—*Tachanun* and Concluding Prayers
7 x 10, 240 pp, Hardcover, ISBN 1-879045-84-2 **$24.95**
Vol. 7—Shabbat at Home
7 x 10, 240 pp, Hardcover, ISBN 1-879045-85-0 **$24.95**
Vol. 8—*Kabbalat Shabbat* (Welcoming Shabbat in the Synagogue)
7 x 10, 240 pp, Hardcover, ISBN 1-58023-121-7 **$24.99**

Spirituality/The Way Into... Series

The Way Into... Series offers an accessible and highly usable "guided tour" of the Jewish faith, people, history and beliefs—in total, an introduction to Judaism that will enable you to understand and interact with the sacred texts of the Jewish tradition. Each volume is written by a leading contemporary scholar and teacher, and explores one key aspect of Judaism. The Way Into... enables all readers to achieve a real sense of Jewish cultural literacy through guided study.

The Way Into Encountering God in Judaism By Neil Gillman
6 x 9, 240 pp, Quality PB, ISBN 1-58023-199-3 **$18.99**; Hardcover, ISBN 1-58023-025-3 **$21.95**

Also Available: **The Jewish Approach to God: A Brief Introduction for Christians**
By Neil Gillman 5½ x 8½, 192 pp, Quality PB, ISBN 1-58023-190-X **$16.95**

The Way Into Jewish Mystical Tradition By Lawrence Kushner
6 x 9, 224 pp, Quality PB, ISBN 1-58023-200-0 **$18.99**; Hardcover, ISBN 1-58023-029-6 **$21.95**

The Way Into Jewish Prayer By Lawrence A. Hoffman
6 x 9, 224 pp, Quality PB, ISBN 1-58023-201-9 **$18.99**; Hardcover, ISBN 1-58023-027-X **$21.95**

The Way Into Torah By Norman J. Cohen
6 x 9, 176 pp, Quality PB, ISBN 1-58023-198-5 **$16.99**; Hardcover, ISBN 1-58023-028-8 **$21.95**

Spirituality in the Workplace

Being God's Partner
How to Find the Hidden Link Between Spirituality and Your Work
By Rabbi Jeffrey K. Salkin. Introduction by Norman Lear.
6 x 9, 192 pp, Quality PB, ISBN 1-879045-65-6 **$17.95**

The Business Bible: 10 New Commandments for Bringing Spirituality & Ethical Values into the Workplace By Rabbi Wayne Dosick
5½ x 8½, 208 pp, Quality PB, ISBN 1-58023-101-2 **$14.95**

Spirituality and Wellness

Aleph-Bet Yoga
Embodying the Hebrew Letters for Physical and Spiritual Well-Being
By Steven A. Rapp. Foreword by Tamar Frankiel, Ph.D., and Judy Greenfeld. Preface by Hart Lazer
7 x 10, 128 pp, b/w photos, Quality PB, Layflat binding, ISBN 1-58023-162-4 **$16.95**

Entering the Temple of Dreams
Jewish Prayers, Movements, and Meditations for the End of the Day
By Tamar Frankiel, Ph.D., and Judy Greenfeld
7 x 10, 192 pp, illus., Quality PB, ISBN 1-58023-079-2 **$16.95**

Jewish Paths toward Healing and Wholeness: A Personal Guide to Dealing with Suffering By Rabbi Kerry M. Olitzky. Foreword by Debbie Friedman.
6 x 9, 192 pp, Quality PB, ISBN 1-58023-068-7 **$15.95**

Minding the Temple of the Soul
Balancing Body, Mind, and Spirit through Traditional Jewish Prayer, Movement, and Meditation By Tamar Frankiel, Ph.D., and Judy Greenfeld
7 x 10, 184 pp, illus., Quality PB, ISBN 1-879045-64-8 **$16.95**
Audiotape of the Blessings and Meditations: 60 min. **$9.95**
Videotape of the Movements and Meditations: 46 min. **$20.00**

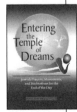

Spirituality/Women's Interest

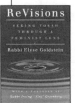

The Quotable Jewish Woman: Wisdom, Inspiration & Humor from
the Mind & Heart *Edited and compiled by Elaine Bernstein Partnow*
The definitive collection of ideas, reflections, humor, and wit of over 300 Jewish women.
6 x 9, 496 pp, Hardcover, ISBN 1-58023-193-4 **$29.99**

Lifecycles, Vol. 1: Jewish Women on Life Passages & Personal Milestones
Edited and with introductions by Rabbi Debra Orenstein 6 x 9, 480 pp, Quality PB, ISBN 1-58023-018-0 **$19.95**

Lifecycles, Vol. 2: Jewish Women on Biblical Themes in Contemporary Life
Edited and with introductions by Rabbi Debra Orenstein and Rabbi Jane Rachel Litman
6 x 9, 464 pp, Quality PB, ISBN 1-58023-019-9 **$19.95**

Moonbeams: A Hadassah Rosh Hodesh Guide *Edited by Carol Diament, Ph.D.*
8½ x 11, 240 pp, Quality PB, ISBN 1-58023-099-7 **$20.00**

ReVisions: Seeing Torah through a Feminist Lens *By Rabbi Elyse Goldstein*
5½ x 8½ , 224 pp, Quality PB, ISBN 1-58023-117-9 **$16.95**

White Fire: A Portrait of Women Spiritual Leaders in America
By Rabbi Malka Drucker. Photographs by Gay Block.
7 x 10, 320 pp, 30+ b/w photos, Hardcover, ISBN 1-893361-64-0 **$24.95** *(A SkyLight Paths book)*

Women of the Wall: Claiming Sacred Ground at Judaism's Holy Site
Edited by Phyllis Chesler and Rivka Haut 6 x 9, 496 pp, b/w photos, Hardcover, ISBN 1-58023-161-6 **$34.95**

The Women's Haftarah Commentary: New Insights from Women Rabbis on
the 54 Weekly Haftarah Portions, the 5 Megillot & Special Shabbatot
Edited by Rabbi Elyse Goldstein 6 x 9, 560 pp, Hardcover, ISBN 1-58023-133-0 **$39.99**

The Women's Torah Commentary: New Insights from Women Rabbis on the 54
Weekly Torah Portions *Edited by Rabbi Elyse Goldstein*
6 x 9, 496 pp, Hardcover, ISBN 1-58023-076-8 **$34.95**

The Year Mom Got Religion: One Woman's Midlife Journey into Judaism
By Lee Meyerhoff Hendler 6 x 9, 208 pp, Quality PB, ISBN 1-58023-070-9 **$15.95**

See Holidays for *The Women's Passover Companion: Women's Reflections on
the Festival of Freedom* and *The Women's Seder Sourcebook: Rituals &
Readings for Use at the Passover Seder.*

Travel

Israel—A Spiritual Travel Guide: A Companion for the Modern Jewish Pilgrim
By Rabbi Lawrence A. Hoffman 4¾ x 10, 256 pp, Quality PB, illus., ISBN 1-879045-56-7 **$18.95**
Also Available: **The Israel Mission Leader's Guide** ISBN 1-58023-085-7 **$4.95**

12 Steps

100 Blessings Every Day
Daily Twelve Step Recovery Affirmations, Exercises for Personal Growth &
Renewal Reflecting Seasons of the Jewish Year
By Rabbi Kerry M. Olitzky. Foreword by Rabbi Neil Gillman.
One-day-at-a-time monthly format. Reflects on the rhythm of the Jewish calen-
dar to bring insight to recovery from addictions.
4½ x 6½, 432 pp, Quality PB, ISBN 1-879045-30-3 **$15.99**

Recovery from Codependence: A Jewish Twelve Steps Guide to Healing Your Soul
By Rabbi Kerry M. Olitzky 6 x 9, 160 pp, Quality PB, ISBN 1-879045-32-X **$13.95**

Renewed Each Day: Daily Twelve Step Recovery Meditations Based on the Bible
By Rabbi Kerry M. Olitzky and Aaron Z.
Vol. 1—Genesis & Exodus: 6 x 9, 224 pp, Quality PB, ISBN 1-879045-12-5 **$14.95**
Vol. 2—Leviticus, Numbers & Deuteronomy: 6 x 9, 280 pp, Quality PB, ISBN 1-879045-13-3 **$14.95**

Twelve Jewish Steps to Recovery: A Personal Guide to Turning from Alcoholism &
Other Addictions—Drugs, Food, Gambling, Sex...
By Rabbi Kerry M. Olitzky and Stuart A. Copans, M.D. Preface by Abraham J. Twerski, M.D.
6 x 9, 144 pp, Quality PB, ISBN 1-879045-09-5 **$14.95**

Theology/Philosophy

Aspects of Rabbinic Theology
By Solomon Schechter. New Introduction by Dr. Neil Gillman.
6 x 9, 448 pp, Quality PB, ISBN 1-879045-24-9 **$19.95**

Broken Tablets: Restoring the Ten Commandments and Ourselves
Edited by Rachel S. Mikva. Introduction by Lawrence Kushner. Afterword by Arnold Jacob Wolf.
6 x 9, 192 pp, Quality PB, ISBN 1-58023-158-6 **$16.95**; Hardcover, ISBN 1-58023-066-0 **$21.95**

Creating an Ethical Jewish Life
A Practical Introduction to Classic Teachings on How to Be a Jew
By Dr. Byron L. Sherwin and Seymour J. Cohen
6 x 9, 336 pp, Quality PB, ISBN 1-58023-114-4 **$19.95**

The Death of Death: Resurrection and Immortality in Jewish Thought
By Dr. Neil Gillman 6 x 9, 336 pp, Quality PB, ISBN 1-58023-081-4 **$18.95**

Evolving Halakhah: A Progressive Approach to Traditional Jewish Law
By Rabbi Dr. Moshe Zemer
6 x 9, 480 pp, Quality PB, ISBN 1-58023-127-6 **$29.95**; Hardcover, ISBN 1-58023-002-4 **$40.00**

Hasidic Tales: Annotated & Explained
By Rabbi Rami Shapiro. Foreword by Andrew Harvey, SkyLight Illuminations series editor.
5½ x 8½, 240 pp, Quality PB, ISBN 1-893361-86-1 **$16.95** *(A SkyLight Paths Book)*

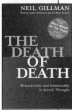

A Heart of Many Rooms: Celebrating the Many Voices within Judaism
By Dr. David Hartman 6 x 9, 352 pp, Quality PB, ISBN 1-58023-156-X **$19.95**

The Hebrew Prophets: Selections Annotated & Explained
Translation & Annotation by Rabbi Rami Shapiro. Foreword by Zalman M. Schachter-Shalomi
5½ x 8½, 224 pp, Quality PB, ISBN 1-59473-037-7 **$16.99** *(A SkyLight Paths book)*

Keeping Faith with the Psalms: Deepen Your Relationship with God Using the
Book of Psalms *By Daniel F. Polish* 6 x 9, 272 pp, Hardcover, ISBN 1-58023-179-9 **$24.95**

The Last Trial
On the Legends and Lore of the Command to Abraham to Offer Isaac as a Sacrifice
By Shalom Spiegel. New Introduction by Judah Goldin.
6 x 9, 208 pp, Quality PB, ISBN 1-879045-29-X **$18.95**

A Living Covenant: The Innovative Spirit in Traditional Judaism
By Dr. David Hartman 6 x 9, 368 pp, Quality PB, ISBN 1-58023-011-3 **$18.95**

Love and Terror in the God Encounter
The Theological Legacy of Rabbi Joseph B. Soloveitchik
By Dr. David Hartman
6 x 9, 240 pp, Quality PB, ISBN 1-58023-176-4 **$19.95**; Hardcover, ISBN 1-58023-112-8 **$25.00**

Seeking the Path to Life
Theological Meditations on God and the Nature of People, Love, Life and Death
By Rabbi Ira F. Stone 6 x 9, 160 pp, Quality PB, ISBN 1-879045-47-8 **$14.95**

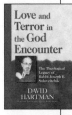

The Spirit of Renewal: Finding Faith after the Holocaust
By Rabbi Edward Feld 6 x 9, 224 pp, Quality PB, ISBN 1-879045-40-0 **$16.95**

Tormented Master: *The Life and Spiritual Quest of Rabbi Nahman of Bratslav*
By Dr. Arthur Green 6 x 9, 416 pp, Quality PB, ISBN 1-879045-11-7 **$19.99**

Your Word Is Fire: The Hasidic Masters on Contemplative Prayer
Edited and translated by Dr. Arthur Green and Barry W. Holtz
6 x 9, 160 pp, Quality PB, ISBN 1-879045-25-7 **$15.95**

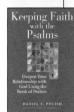

I Am Jewish
Personal Reflections Inspired by the Last Words of Daniel Pearl
Almost 150 Jews—both famous and not—from all walks of life, from all around
the world, write about Identity, Heritage, Covenant / Chosenness and Faith,
Humanity and Ethnicity, and *Tikkun Olam* and Justice.
Edited by Judea and Ruth Pearl
6 x 9, 304 pp, Hardcover, ISBN 1-58023-183-7 **$24.99**

Download a free copy of the *I Am Jewish Teacher's Guide* at our website:
www.jewishlights.com

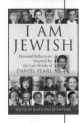

About Jewish Lights

People of all faiths and backgrounds yearn for books that attract, engage, educate, and spiritually inspire.

Our principal goal is to stimulate thought and help all people learn about who the Jewish People are, where they come from, and what the future can be made to hold. While people of our diverse Jewish heritage are the primary audience, our books speak to people in the Christian world as well and will broaden their understanding of Judaism and the roots of their own faith.

We bring to you authors who are at the forefront of spiritual thought and experience. While each has something different to say, they all say it in a voice that you can hear.

Our books are designed to welcome you and then to engage, stimulate, and inspire. We judge our success not only by whether or not our books are beautiful and commercially successful, but by whether or not they make a difference in your life.

For your information and convenience, at the back of this book we have provided a list of other Jewish Lights books you might find interesting and useful. They cover all the categories of your life:

Bar/Bat Mitzvah
Bible Study / Midrash
Children's Books
Congregation Resources
Current Events / History
Ecology
Fiction: Mystery, Science Fiction
Grief / Healing
Holidays / Holy Days
Inspiration
Kabbalah / Mysticism / Enneagram

Life Cycle
Meditation
Parenting
Prayer
Ritual / Sacred Practice
Spirituality
Theology / Philosophy
Travel
Twelve Steps
Women's Interest

Stuart M. Matlins, Publisher

Or phone, fax, mail or e-mail to: **JEWISH LIGHTS Publishing**
Sunset Farm Offices, Route 4 • P.O. Box 237 • Woodstock, Vermont 05091
Tel: (802) 457-4000 • Fax: (802) 457-4004 • www.jewishlights.com
Credit card orders: **(800) 962-4544** (8:30AM–5:30PM ET Monday–Friday)
Generous discounts on quantity orders. SATISFACTION GUARANTEED. Prices subject to change.

For more information about each book, visit our website at www.jewishlights.com